Buddhism, Imperialism and War

Buddhism, Imperialism and War

Burma and Thailand in modern history

TREVOR LING

Professor of Comparative Religion,
University of Manchester

London
GEORGE ALLEN & UNWIN
Boston   Sydney

First published in 1979

GEORGE ALLEN & UNWIN LTD .
40 Museum Street, London WC1A 1LU

©George Allen & Unwin (Publishers) Ltd, 1979

British Library Cataloguing in Publication Data

Ling, Trevor
    Buddhism, imperialism and war.
    1. Buddhism and state – Burma – History
    2. Burma – Politics and government   3. Buddhism
    and state – Thailand – History   4. Thailand –
    Politics and government
    I. Title
    294.3′3′7709591   BQ420   79–40378

ISBN 0-04-294105-9

Typeset in 10 on 11 point Plantin by Northampton Phototypesetters Ltd
and printed in Great Britain
by Billing & Sons Ltd, Guildford, London and Worcester

to

EDWARD CONZE

who disagrees like a true friend

Contents

Introduction

There is a small but growing body of literature on the attitudes of the major religions of the world to peace and war. Buddhism in theory gives a high place to the maintenance of peace, both between individuals and between social groups. Buddhist nations in practice, however, are no strangers to the battlefield. They have frequently been found there, sometimes engaged in war with would-be conquerors and sometimes in aggressive imperial exploits of their own. In both cases Buddhist nation has been found warring against Buddhist nation.

This raises the question: what is a 'Buddhist' nation? Large issues are involved here and, although these cannot be fully explored, the intention is at least to indicate some of the complexity which underlies the superficially simple idea that Burma, for example, and Thailand are, alike, 'Buddhist' nations. Some preliminary remarks at this point may help to place the narrative which follows in a conceptual framework, albeit of a provisional kind which may need to be revised later.

The relationship between a particular religious community and other elements in society can, in the modern world, be a matter of some importance. A 'religious community' can be any one of the various types of religious organisation such as cults, sects, denominations and churches, or a state religion. Very few forms of religious belief and practice exist entirely without any supporting and surrounding community within which the beliefs are preserved and transmitted and the practices are observed. It is true that religious belief, at least, and possibly even practice of some sort, does not absolutely require the existence of a community; there has recently been a growing recognition, by Thomas Luckman and others, of a type of non-institutional belief which he has called 'The Invisible Religion' and which Robert Towler has called 'Common Religion' (111). Nevertheless, the practice of religion frequently results in the formation of a community or collectivity of some kind.

The relationship between such religious communities or collectivities on the one hand and other social groups and interests on the other can be fraught with tension and conflict, or it can assist integration and harmony. One of the crucial factors in the situation is the attitude of the political rulers towards religion. In a state which gives preferential treatment to one religion, there is likely to be conflict with the other, non-privileged and often non-conforming religious groups. In a state where the official policy is an open religious pluralism, and where serious continuous efforts are made to implement such a policy, as in the United States and India, religious collectivities are *less* likely to act as disintegratory forces (unless one of those religious collectivities has also certain inbuilt political ambitions which are essential to its nature).

The study of such relationships can best be furthered by the comparative investigation of a wide range of examples and types of situation. A contribution to comparative study of this kind has now become possible on the basis of data from Burma and Thailand. One of the advantages of this particular comparison is that the number of independent variables is reduced by the fact that both countries have similar environments and both have been to some extent influenced by the Theravada school of Buddhism. The differences between them are partly ethnic and cultural, and partly political. The political differences arise partly out of the history of the modern period, but not entirely. I have attempted to provide a comparative as well as a synoptic account of Buddhist culture in these two countries, although only of an introductory kind, it must be emphasised.

Thailand was never a European colony. This, it is said repeatedly, is one of the great advantages the Thais had over their neighbours. Such freedom may appear to have given Thailand the opportunity to advance more rapidly towards modernisation. How far Thailand has been successful in preserving Buddhist values and attitudes while doing so, is, however, another matter. It may be true in a very general sense that the emergence of modern society has entailed both the establishment of new intellectual or 'spiritual' attitudes and the decline of traditional religious beliefs and attitudes. But what is perhaps more important for us to try to understand, towards the end of the twentieth century, is what Ernest Gellner has called, not these grand processes as such, but 'the mechanics of a transition' (25:20). In this comparison of Thailand and Burma we are concerned with the transition from medieval to modern, and the contrasting condition of Buddhism as it emerges in the modern period.

xii

In Burma, which was subjected to imperial rule by Britain and then became independent in 1947, Buddhism is said to have languished because of the disruption of the traditional pattern of state Buddhism caused by British rule. If the latter assertion is true it follows that Buddhism is a religious system of such a kind that it is likely to be at a severe disadvantage in the modern 'secular' (or religiously non-aligned) state, such as India. This study will include a critical examination of this line of argument. 'Religion, King and Country' is the slogan of today's Thai state, ruled by its military elite.

The interconnections existing within this holy trio, to whose preservation the Thai state is dedicated, demand closer scrutiny than they have received in the past.

Many states have, in the past, nationalised one of the religions practised by the citizens. England did so in the early modern period, and has not yet completely undone the nationalisation measure passed in 1662. But none perhaps has nationalised religion so thoroughly and efficiently as modern Thailand. Neighbouring Burma may have been travelling a parallel road in the eighteenth century, but after that it was deflected by the obstacles placed in its way by the irruption of British imperial rule.

In Thailand the nationalisation of Buddhist religion has entailed the transformation of its symbols into Thai national symbols. This came about as the result of a long process of development over several centuries of recent history. Buddhist symbols had been nationalised before, notably in Sri Lanka, especially in the medieval period, in what has been called the Buddhist revival under King Parakamma Bahu in the eleventh century. The model for the *kind* of Buddhist state set up then in Sri Lanka is often said to be that of the Asokan state in ancient India, almost at the beginning of Buddhist history. But it is arguable that too much has been read into the religious history of Asoka's India from later, medieval situations, particularly that of Sri Lanka.

Undoubtedly there was much that was attractive both to kings and to monks in the kind of arrangement which was developed in the various countries of Asia where Buddhism established itself, in the reciprocal relationship whereby the king protected and supported the monkhood and the monks legitimated royal rule by endowing it with ethical meaning and by acting as agents of social control through their advocacy of attitudes of peaceableness, gentleness, and obedience among the common people. But there was also some danger to the central principles of Buddhist teaching and practice, which, it is possible to see, has now become acute in Thailand. This danger was hinted at in a number of the utterances attributed to the Buddha in the India of the sixth century BC, but these warnings about what we may call the debit side of monarchy were too easily set aside (just as those of the prophet Samuel were in ancient Israel) in circumstances where the pressures were strong in the direction of a Sangha-and-King *entente*. In order to see medieval and modern developments in Buddhist Thailand and Burma in proper perspective some knowledge of the early development of Buddhism in India is necessary. However, it is not the purpose of the present book to convey that kind of information; for that the reader may be referred to my earlier work, *The Buddha : Buddhist Civilization in India and Ceylon.**

The religious aspect of life in Burma is predominantly Buddhist. That is to say, in Burma the most commonly observed features of religion appear to be Buddhist rather than, say, Islamic. This predominant flavour is, however, always open to change as new ideologies claim the attention of at least some of the people. It has changed in the past. One of the most notable changes in the late medieval period was the increase in the amount of Sinhalese, Pali Buddhism present in Burma. This altered the predominant flavour from what had previously been a blend of spirit and demon worship, astrology, meditational practices and Mahayana Buddhist ideas of bodhisattvas into a blend of spirit and demon worship, astrology, messianic cults, ethical precepts, meditational practices, and Buddhist bibliolatry. This, as the work of Michael Mendelson has served to bring to the attention of students of Burmese religion, is mainly what Burmese Buddhism has consisted of right into the modern period. But the flavour is always changing, very slightly and very slowly, as new ideological ingredients are added. In the modern period Protestantism, socialism, Marxism, and, particularly, nationalism have been the major new ingredients in Burma.

A similar but by no means identical blend is found in neighbouring Thailand. The only appropriate name that can be applied to this blend is 'Thai Buddhism'. Both Burmese Buddhism and Thai Buddhism have certain features in common. Orthodox Pali textual scholars tend to see only the fact that Pali texts are

*Pelican Books, 1976.

housed in the monasteries of Burma and Thailand, and that a certain number of monks can read and understand them; beyond this, however, such scholars tend to ignore the other, differential ingredients, so that the view has become fairly widespread that the religion of both Burma and Thailand is 'Theravada (or Pali) Buddhism'.

Discovering what *is* the 'religion' of any large number of people is a difficult problem, as an English anthropologist, Rodney Needham, has pointed out. It is extremely difficult to make large-scale statements about the beliefs of whole peoples. When the difficulties are ignored and such statements are nevertheless made they are likely to be so misleading as to be worse than useless.

If they are assertions about the inner states of individuals, as by common usage they would normally be taken to be, then, so far as my acquaintance with the literature goes, no evidence of such states, as distinct from the collective representations that are thus recorded, is ever presented, writes Needham. There is no point, moreover, as he goes on to say, in speaking of collective representations, or dogmas which are true of a culture as a whole, as 'beliefs' if it is not implied that the individual human beings who compose the social aggregate in question actually and severally believe (73:5f).

We simply cannot say with any degree of reliability what the beliefs of the Burmese or the Thai people are. We can, however, ascertain what their society and their culture have trained them to *say* they believe. This will vary from time to time in the same society, as the dominant social, economic, ecclesiastical and political forces change. In the cases of Burma and Thailand it is possible to study the changes in these dominant forces and get some general notion of how they have differed in the two cases. This study is therefore primarily historical, and will be concerned largely with the more public aspects of Burmese and Thai life in the modern period. By this is meant the period from about the beginning of the sixteenth century, when the European presence in South-East Asia began to be felt. The intention is to enable the reader to become more familiar with the ways in which Burma's historical development has conditioned Burma's people to articulate their attitudes and beliefs in certain ways, and in which on the other hand Thai history has conditioned Thai people to give a somewhat different public account of their attitudes and beliefs. The culture in both cases can be broadly characterised as 'Buddhist', subject to the qualifications 'Burmese' and 'Thai' respectively. There is, that is to say, common ground, and there are contrasts. The present book thus attempts to indicate some approaches to the understanding of the common ground and the contrasts. In that sense it may serve as an introduction to the kind of comparative cultural study which can with profit be carried out in other cases of similar but by no means identical cultural communities; it may also serve to clarify the extent to which religious ideals affect (or do not affect) the public and political life of the society in which they may be theoretically honoured.

Of the ancient Khmer civilisation Arnold Toynbee wrote that 'like so many civilisations before and after it, it wrecked itself' by its 'mad crimes', that is its imperialistic wars. The Khmer empire itself was eventually engulfed in that of the Thais. The latter was continually subject to attack from the expanding empire of Burma. The Burmese empire, in its turn, fell a victim to the rapaciousness of the British merchants of Rangoon. Fed by an overweening ambition to set its bounds 'wider still and wider' the empire of Victorian Britain collapsed by the middle of the twentieth century, exhausted, overstretched and unable to contain any longer the rising tide of nationalism in so many of the territories it occupied. Some of this serial story is the subject-matter of the present book, and it may not be entirely irrelevant to what is happening elsewhere in the world today, and what may happen tomorrow.

Burma, Thailand, and neighbouring lands

Buddhism, Imperialism and War

I

Early Buddhist
Burma and Thailand

The terrain and its peoples

The modern political divisions of Indianised mainland South-East Asia, namely Burma, Thailand, Laos, Cambodia and Malaysia, have little relevance to the region as it was during the pre-modern period. During the centuries when Buddhism was declining in India and advancing in South-East Asia, the people of the latter area were divided along political and cultural lines which run right across the boundaries of today. In the south of Burma and of Thailand were the Mon people. In the eastern half of what is now Thailand and in Cambodia were the Khmers. In the central and northern part of Burma were the Pyu and Burmese peoples, who had entered the region from the north-west. In the east of modern Burma and the northern parts of Thailand were the various branches of the Thai people, who had entered the region from the north-east.

Besides these broadly 'ethnic' divisions there is another important distinguishing feature which runs right through South-East Asia, and that is the distinction between valley and hill peoples. The whole region may be characterised as a complex series of roughly parallel ranges of mountains running in a north–south direction, with about four or five major river valleys (Irrawaddy, Sittang, Salween, Menam and Mekong), also following a generally north–south direction, except for the Mekong whose course from the mountains of Yunnan to its delta in South Vietnam is roughly from north–west to south–east, and which in its central reaches, where it forms the frontier between Thailand and Laos, is mostly in a west–east direction.

I

Thus, the physical and social background to Buddhist culture in Burma and Thailand is in certain of its basic features similar to the kind associated with the rise of Buddhism in India (51:44ff). The physical setting is similar; there are extensive riverine plains, having either a sufficiently heavy monsoon rainfall to make wet rice cultivation possible, or an all-year flow of water in snow-fed rivers, thus making it possible by means of irrigation, as in the dry zone of the central Irrawaddy valley in Burma. In Indochina, as in India, there is a significant difference between the economy of the river valleys and that of the neighbouring uplands. In the river valleys wet rice cultivation provides an abundance of food in the form of both rice and the abundant fish which live in this watery countryside. In other words, there was, for many centuries, in the valleys, a subsistence economy where a substantial surplus could be obtained without difficulty and with minimal intensity of labour. In the adjacent hills where rice is grown with more difficulty such surpluses are less likely, and far less common. This difference has important cultural consequences, and appears to some extent to limit the geographical area in which the institutional form of Theravada Buddhism can spread freely. Even where, on a small-scale map, Buddhism appears to be present in a hilly region, such as in the Shan States of Burma, or in north Thailand, it will be found on closer examination that the towns and villages are located in the narrow alluvial valleys, where wet rice can be grown, and are surrounded by high, thickly forested ridges. It is in these villages of the river valleys that Buddhism has been established.

One of the major differences between the hill and valley peoples of Indochina is that by reason of their association with China some of the hill people have been open to continuing Chinese commercial and social influences, whereas the valley peoples, because of their early association with India by sea, received the patterns of their social, religious and political institutions from India (89:24). The valley people, moreover, with their more prosperous and settled agricultural life, have tended to regard the hill peoples as barbarians. The existence of an agricultural surplus has made more easily possible the support of the Sangha in the valley regions. It has also made possible the existence of at least one city in each major area from which the political administration of the area could be carried out, because it provided sufficient surplus for the economic support of a ruler and his officers. The conditions are thus of a kind to favour the establishment of the characteristically Buddhist pattern of civilisation, in which king, Sangha and people are the three principal and mutually supporting elements; it is also a situation in which a general awareness of the nature of the human situation, closely similar to that found among the people of the Gangetic plain at the time of the Buddha, is likely to develop.

Buddhist beginnings in Burma and Thailand

It is known that the early Buddhists of India had a strong inclination to carry their religion, and with it their civilisation, into the lands which lay beyond their immediate frontiers. There is a tradition, recorded in the Pali chronicles, that the Indian emperor Asoka sent missions to various places which bordered on his empire. One of these, to the east, is called in the Pali chronicles Suvannabhumi (Golden Land). There is mention also of a place called Suvannadipa (Golden Island), somewhere in the same direction. After a great deal of debate opinion has settled down to giving these names a fairly wide general reference, roughly equivalent to Indochina and the Indonesian archipelago respectively. Modern usage has accustomed us to thinking of hard and fast lines dividing from India all those lands to the east, which we think of not as Indian but as Burmese, Thai, Malayan, etc. However, as G. Coedès points out, the Indianisation of the cultures of Indochina did not differ essentially from the Indianisation of the indigenous cultures of the subcontinent itself (16:55). Or, to put it another way, as Vallée Poussin pointed out, it is no more than 'the extension overseas of the process of Brahmanization which started long before the time of the Buddha, and which, from its area of origin in North-West India, has spread and still continues to spread in Bengal and the south' (16:55). The only difference between the Aryanisation of, say, Bengal and that of Burma and Thailand is that the first was a process of gradual diffusion across the country, district by district, village by village, whereas the second was a process which took place partly by sea, across the Bay of Bengal. Even so, this too was partly an overland process. A route used by traders passed through Assam, upper Burma and Yunnan into China, and there is evidence of Indian culture, including Mahayana Buddhism, having reached upper Burma by this route during the seventh century CE (16:113). Evidence from the Mae Khlong river valley route and the Three Pagodas Pass, between Burma and Thailand, indicates that over-

3

land routes across the Indochina peninsula were used earlier than the fifth century CE (116:4, 14).

It is thus perfectly proper, from a cultural point of view, to regard Indian civilisation as extending eastwards not merely, say, as far as Chittagong or Manipur, but to Mandalay, to Moulmein, to Bangkok and to Phnom Penh. From a modern political point of view this is less apparent.

It is generally agreed that there was also an infiltration of South Indians by sea into the coastal areas of South-East Asia during the early centuries of the Christian era. The coast of Burma is largely inhospitable and is lashed by the fury of the south-west monsoon for four months of the year. But when the Irrawaddy delta is reached, with its flat shores lying behind the outliers of the Arakan Yoma which form the western coast, some shelter is to be found in the major distributory channels of the Irrawaddy and, here and there, places to harbour. Specialists in the history of ancient South-East Asia have suggested that it was Buddhism alone which blazed the trail by which Indian civilisation and culture crossed the seas eastwards from India, even though in the later stages it was not only Buddhism but also Brahmanism which was thus transmitted, the latter finding its way especially to the courts of kings.

The wide, green plain of what is now central and western Thailand and southern Burma could once have been called 'Mon-land'. For this was, from about the sixth to the eleventh century CE, the land of the Mons, a people who were evidently Buddhists. They called their kingdoms by Indian names such as Dvaravati, for it was from India that they had received their Buddhist religion and culture. The Mons had at some time before the sixth century moved south from the interior of the Asian mainland, down the Salween valley, spreading out westwards into what is now Burma and eastwards into the plain of Thailand. They adopted Buddhist religion and culture from Indian settlers in the region who were known as 'Telinganas', a name which indicates that the settlers had come from the coastal region of south India somewhere in the vicinity of Madras.

The land of the Mons was therefore, in a cultural sense, part of Indian Asia, as is indicated by the Sanskrit name Dvaravati, which was applied to the area that is now the central plain of Thailand; and the Mon states in what is now lower Burma, Rammanadesa (modern Pegu), and the neighbouring state of Sudhammavati (modern Thaton).

4

It was in these Mon states that Pali Buddhism was first planted in South-East Asia, and it was from these states that it spread to other peoples of the area. We shall therefore look briefly at the main features of this cultural encounter with the migrant Burmese and Thai peoples coming into the area from various lands to the north.

In the seventh century, when the Chinese pilgrim Huien-Tsang was travelling in India and observing some of the signs of Buddhism's decline, the Mon kingdom of Dvaravati was already advancing to the special kind of greatness which has been recognised in its history, that of upholding the spiritual ideals of Buddhism (116:1). The kingdom was known to the Chinese as To-lo-po-ti, according to Huien-Tsang. Its centre was at Lopburi, on the lower Menam river. Buddhist texts in Pali have been found at this site. Also found here was the Wat San Sung pillar (now in the Vajiranana Library in Bangkok), on which are the oldest known Mon inscriptions, dating from the latter part of the eighth century.

Another centre of the Mons was evidently at Nakhon Pathom, in the Menam plain about forty miles west of the modern Bangkok. Fragments of inscriptions in archaic Mon language have been found here as well as at Lopburi. The Nakhon Pathom inscription is probably sixth-century and that from Lopburi is seventh-century. Moreover, there is at Nakhon Pathom the remains of a stupa, or Buddhist shrine, of an obviously very early style, together with Buddhist symbols in stone, in the shape of a wheel, together with statues of deer, suggesting the theme of the Buddha's setting in motion the wheel of the Dhamma in the Deer Park at Benares. A little farther to the west similar stupa foundations have been discovered, and *Buddha-rupas*, or statues, in the Gupta style of India, that is of the fourth century CE and later.

The Pyu people are the earliest known of several waves of Tibeto–Burman migrants who moved into South–East Asia from the mountainous region of eastern Tibet. The first known mention of them is in certain Chinese texts of the Tsin dynasty (265–420 CE) which refer to the Pyus as wild and disorderly tribes living in the mountains on China's Burma border; they tattooed themselves, and some were cannibals, with 'the curious habit of feeding their guests on the elderly relatives of their next-door neighbours' (56:24). Moving into Burma down the Irrawaddy valley, they came into contact with the Mons and with Buddhism in the seventh century. They had, by the time that happened, reached the area of modern Prome, at the head of the Irrawaddy delta. Here they founded a new capital, which became known by the Indian name of Sri Ksetra, or City of Splendour.

The Pyus appear to have adopted Buddhist religion from the Mons. Evidence from near the site of Sri Ksetra indicates that they must, in the course of time, have gained a considerable knowledge of Pali Buddhism (103:273). In 1926 archaeologists working in the Prome area found 'two gold plates bearing Buddhist Pali texts in a script closely resembling the Pallava script in use in Conjevaram (Kanchipuram) on the eastern seaboard of South India' (3:26). The texts contain Buddhist formulae and ascriptions of praise to the Buddha found in the Pali canonical text, the *Anguttara Nikaya* (83:29). At another site near Prome two large gold statues of the Buddha were discovered, together with a silver relic-casket bearing inscriptions in Pali in a south-Indian script closely similar to that of Kanchipuram. The casket also bears representations of the Buddha in the style of the Theravadin school (54:48).

By the seventh century the Pyu kingdom of Sri Ksetra had become famous in the Buddhist world. It is recorded that the Chinese pilgrim Huien-Tsang, standing on the seashore in Bengal and looking across the water, inquired what Buddhists there were in the lands to the south—east of Bengal. One of the places mentioned was Sri Ksetra and, although he could not visit it, he recorded its name in his travel diary.

Soon after 718, when the last king of Sri Ksetra died, the Pyus appear to have been forced back from the Prome area further inland to a new capital at Halingyi, south of Shwebo. A Chinese chronicle of the T'ang dynasty, in a chapter on 'Southern Barbarians', provides a lengthy description of the Pyu state about 800 CE. We are told that when the Pyu king went out he was carried on a couch of gold cord; for travelling long distances he used an elephant. The city was walled and had twelve gates and the area enclosed was about five and a half square miles (30:12). The people lived in the confines of the walls, and, says the chronicler, disliked taking life. For this reason they avoided wearing silk, as it entailed taking the life of the silkworm. 'They are Buddhists and have a hundred monasteries, with bricks of glass ware embellished with gold and silver vermillion, gay colours and red kino . . . . At seven years of age the people cut their hair and enter a monastery.' This was apparently for the period of their education, which lasted until they were twenty. If by that time they had become masters of Buddhist doctrine they remained in the monastery (30:13).

It is clear from the wealth of Pali inscriptions found near Prome that the Pyu kingdom from the fifth to the tenth century CE was an important centre of Theravada Buddhism, and that this had been transmitted from south India. Pali, the language of Theravada Buddhism, was apparently known and understood by at least some of the inhabitants of the capital city and the study of Pali canonical texts was carried out at a fairly advanced level.

Another important event of the seventh century (approximately 649) was the founding of the kingdom of Nanchao in Yunnan, in south-western China. This was a Thai kingdom, and was destined to form a kind of reservoir of the Thai peoples who would subsequently migrate from here outwards to Assam, Manipur, Upper Burma, the Shan States of eastern Burma, and, most of all, to what is now Thailand. The kingdom of Nanchao was set up in independence of the empire of China. Like other non-Chinese peoples the Thais are referred to in Chinese records as 'the barbarians'. In this case, they were the barbarians who lived to the south of the upper reaches of the Yangtze Kiang. It was in order to remove themselves from the threat of Chinese domination, either political or cultural, or both, that they moved into the mountains, south–westwards. According to a modern Thai historian, Prince Dhani Nivat, their migration began about twelve centuries ago and continued for some centuries after that. He is inclined to accept as the reason for their migration 'their inability to stem the harassing tide of Chinese cultural if not military pressure' (20:3f). According to Louis Finot, 'the march of this strange race being supple and fluid like water insinuating itself with the same force taking the colour of ̦all the skies and the form of all the river banks but keeping the essential identity of its character and language under different aspects, has spread out like an immense sheet from south China, Tongking, Laos, Siam, to Burma and Assam' (99:13). On linguistic grounds the old idea of the affinity of Thai and Chinese has been abandoned. Paul Benedict's analysis has demonstrated that, linguistically, the closer genetic linkage is between Thai and Indonesian rather than Thai and Chinese (92:3); what there is of the latter linkage is of a kind which can be explained as borrowings during the period the Thais were to some extent influenced by Chinese culture. However, the migration of the Thais into the land which now bears their name did not begin until a few centuries later. There was, on the other hand, a migration of some of the Mons northwards, from Lopburi in the Menam plain to found a colony called Haripunjaya in the northern valley region around what is now Lampun. This occurred, according to a legend which is well supported by facts (55:2), under the leadership of a Mon queen of Lopburi named Camadevi in the eighth century. In this way Mon Buddhist culture and religion was, so to speak, advancing to meet the Thais in their subsequent migration southwards.

The Pyus virtually disappear from the scene in the ninth century. In 832 the kingdom of Nanchao sacked the Pyu capital and took some of them away captive to Nanchao. Very soon after this the Burmese* appeared. They had been moving southwards from the lands to the east of Tibet during the eighth century and had themselves become subject to Nanchao. It has been conjectured that it was the Burmese desire to escape from this domination which caused them to move further south.

They were at this time, according to Luce, wild jungle tribes. Descending from the Shan hills into the Irrawaddy they conquered and occupied the fertile plain around Kyaukse, near the confluence of the Irrawaddy and the Chindwin (55:2). Those Pyus who were left in the area appear to have intermingled with these incoming Burmese, until eventually the Pyus were absorbed.

It was from the time of their settlement in the plain that the Burmese came into contact with the Mons and with Buddhism. As in many such cases of the conquest of a more advanced culture by a relatively unsophisticated people, the victors sat at the feet of the vanquished. Luce argues from the linguistic evidence provided by Mon loan-words in Old Burmese that the Burmese 'learnt Indian cults – Brahmanism as well as Buddhism – from the Mons, probably the Mons of Kyaukse' (55: 3). Indian culture had reached Burma by land, by way of the trade route from India to China, which, as we have noted, passed through Assam and upper Burma. Brahman and Mahayana cults probably came by this route. According to Coedès it was in the seventh century, that is about two centuries before the arrival of the Burmese in this area, that Mahayana Buddhism was introduced into the Irrawaddy valley, a form of Mahayana characterised by strongly Tantric practices (16:13). The Burmese built a fortified city on the east bank of the Irrawaddy river just below

---

*The name 'Burman' denotes a citizen of Burma. The word 'Burmese' denotes one particular linguistic group among others, and those whose language is Burmese (as distinct from, e.g., Karens, etc.).

its confluence with the Chindwin. This new capital, Pagan, is said to have occupied the area covered by nineteen villages, each of which had its own Nat, or protector spirit. The ruins of the city are impressive, and testify to its great extent. The traditional date of its founding is 849, but this may be the date of its fortification by means of an enclosing wall.

Buddhism and the Thais

Some Thais, migrating south from the mountains of the Nanchao region in the south-west of China had by the beginning of the thirteenth century settled in the upper part of the Menam plain where it is fairly narrow, between hills to the east and west. When the Thais moved into the lowland area they came under the rule of the Khmers, who at that time dominated the whole of the central plain westwards from Cambodia. Another branch of the southward and westward-migrating Thais came into the hills east of the Irrawaddy and formed communities which bear the name of Shan; these are now a part of Burma. Those who reached the central Menam plain encountered, besides the Khmers, the Buddhist Mons of the kingdom of Haripunjaya. By soon after the middle of the thirteenth century Thai influence extended southwards as far as the Malay peninsula, and down to the borders of the empire of Sri Vijaya, which had its centre in what is now Sumatra.

In 1254 Kublai Khan's conquest of the Nanchao kingdom in the south-west of China had the effect of sending a fresh wave of Thai immigrants south from Nanchao; particularly those who preferred not to remain under Chinese rule but to be free or '*Thai*'. This influx of Thais into the upper Menam valley provided the Thai settlers already there with fresh recruits, and thus increased their ability to control the area. This, as Pendleton points out, really signalised that the Thais had 'arrived'. That is to say it indicated 'their arrival as an independent, politically active, expansive and energetic people' (78:11).

What is important about Thai ascendancy from the second half of the thirteenth century onwards, however, is not only the increasing number of migrant Thais but also the growth of Thai leadership and political rule throughout the territory which is now known as Thailand. This came about perhaps as a consequence not only of the decline of the Mon and Khmer kingdoms in the area but also of the vigour and energy of individual Thai leaders. It was, as Coedès sees it, 'a change in the membership of the ruling classes [rather than] a sudden disruption of the pattern of settlement' (16:131).

Thus, around the year 1260, the town of Sukhodaya in the central Menam plain was part of the Hindu Shaivite and Buddhist Mahayana Khmer kingdom; it was the headquarters of a province under a Khmer governor, but among the people of the province there were by this time a large number of Thais. The son of one of the more outstanding of these became an official under the Khmer administration. With the help of another Thai chief named Bang Klang Tao he carried out a coup and gained political control of Sukhodaya from the Khmer governor. He thereupon set up Bang Klang Tao as the king of the newly formed Thai state of Sukhodaya, the first forerunner of modern Thailand.

At roughly the same time, about two hundred miles to the north, a leader of the Thai Lao tribe, a man named Mangrai, set up his headquarters, which he called Chieng Rai, on a tributary of the upper Mekong river, in the hills of the extreme north of Thailand. Having established himself here, he began extending his control of the area to the south-west, and eventually, after about twenty years, he took over Lampang, the capital of the surviving Mon state of Haripunjaya, and with it control of that state. This became part of an enlarged kingdom of Chieng Rai, and in 1296 he founded a new capital between Chieng Rai and Lampang and called it 'the new city', or Chiengmai, destined later to become (as it is today) the second city of Thailand.

The new Thai state of Sukhodaya, in the Menam plain, soon began to extend the area of its control, especially during the time of its third king, Rama Kamhaeng, that is from 1270 onwards. It was during this period that the Thai state came into contact with a strong centre of Pali Buddhism in the south, in the kingdom of Tambralinga. The situation to the south of Thailand was as follows. The Malay kingdom of Sri Vijaya, which had its capital in northern Sumatra, at Djambi (near Palembang), was now declining in power; at its northern extremity was the separate kingdom of Tambralinga, the capital of which was Ligor (its Malay name; Nakhon Sithammarat is its modern Thai name). Tambralinga, after having been subject to Sri Vijaya at an earlier period (from the eighth to the twelfth century, and then to the Khmer kingdom of Cambodia), had in the mid-thirteenth century become independent again. Now the state of Tambralinga seems to have been a great centre of Pali Buddhism; there is reference to this in a Thai inscription set up by the third king of Sukhodaya, Rama Ramkhaeng. Knowledge and study of Pali Buddhist texts in Tambralinga may either have originated in the twelfth century or have had a fresh stimulus at that time. In either case the cause is likely to have been the revival of Theravada Buddhism in Ceylon brought about in the twelfth century by King Parakamma Bahu (51:191ff). The fame of this revival spread to various other countries of Asia which were in touch with Ceylon; among these was the Malayan kingdom of Tambralinga. Thus it was that bhikkhus returning from Ceylon to Ligor, the capital of Tambralinga, taught there the Buddhism which they had studied in Ceylon (99:27).

It seems to have been from Ligor that the Sinhalese influence spread to the Sukhodaya kingdom during the reign of Rama Kamhaeng. All the active and energetic qualities which characterised the Thai people appear to have been embodied in this king, under whom the political power and influence of the new state of Sukhodaya grew very rapidly. Among the regions to which his influence began to be extended was Ligor. It appears that in the course of a tour of the Malay peninsula he visited Ligor and thus encountered the Sinhalese tradition of Buddhism. It is unlikely that he would have been entirely ignorant of Theravada Buddhism before this, since the former Mon kingdom of Haripunjaya which bordered his own, with which he had cordial relations, was already and had for long been a preserver and transmitter of the Theravada tradition, which the Mons had received from south India. What he encountered in Ligor, however, was the recently renovated and restimulated Sinhalese tradition of state Buddhism (21:287). As a result Rama Kamhaeng invited to his capital at Sukhodaya a very learned and highly esteemed bhikkhu from Ligor. Reference to this is made in an inscription which records how Rama Kamhaeng installed this 'venerable preceptor' in a monastery near the city. It reads as follows: 'To the west of this city of Sukhodaya there is a monastery of the forest monks. King Rama Kamhaeng founded and offered it to the venerable preceptor, learned in all the Tipitaka, in erudition excelling all other monks in the whole land. He hailed from Nakorn Sri Dharmaraj' (modern spelling Nakhon Sithammarat) (20:5). By 1292 Rama Kamhaeng had succeeded in adding this city, and the territory of which it was the capital, to the kingdom of Sukhodaya. The fact is referred to in an inscription of that date by Rama Kamhaeng. The king of Tambralinga was, however, allowed to retain his own style and dignity.

Thus, by the end of the thirteenth century the Thais had gained political sovereignty over the whole area from Chiengmai in the north to Nakhon Sithammaret in the south, and were gradually extending further eastwards into territory formerly controlled by the Khmers, including parts of modern Laos (Luang Prabang and Vientiane). In the west Thai political rule, direct or indirect, extended over the Mon territories of Tenasserim, Tavoy, Martaban and Pegu (now in Burma).

Rama Kamhaeng's influence was notable in other spheres also. He is remembered as the inaugurator of the Thai alphabet, which he devised from the Mon and Khmer scripts. It was this alphabet which was used in the inscription of 1292. The evidence suggests also that he was familiar with Pali language, and this is likely also on other grounds, in particular Rama Kamhaeng's strong personal devotion to Theravada Buddhism (99:27). He showed an active concern for the welfare of the various peoples within the territory over which he had authority, whether they were Thai, Khmer, Mon, Malay, Burmese or Chinese. He had a large bell set up at the palace gate, and whoever wished to submit a complaint rang the bell and gained an audience of the king, who guaranteed that he would hear and attend to all such complaints from the people of his territory. He persuaded the citizens of Sukhodaya to attend the expositions of the Dhamma given by monks on Buddhist holy days from a special seat or throne which the king had erected in a palm grove. The remains of many old wats, or monasteries, at Sukhodaya are evidence of the extent to which Buddhism had been promoted in Rama Kamhaeng's kingdom.

Not only had Thai ascendency in what is now Thailand been established, but Pali Buddhism had also become the characteristic form of monastic life. The loss of influence by the Khmers and the kingdom of Sri Vijaya entailed also the decline of Hindu Shaivite and Vaishnavite and Buddhist Mahayana cults; the growth of Thai influence meant a corresponding increase in adherence to the Pali Buddhism of Sinhalese origin. Writing from the perspective of the middle of the fourteenth century, a later king of Sukhodaya, Lu Thai, in an inscription made in 1357, recorded that great changes had been seen over the previous hundred years or more. From about that time 'the nobles and the high dignitaries, the Brahmans and the wealthy merchants gradually ceased to occupy the first place in society; also from that time, astrologers and physicians lost their prestige, from that time on they were no longer respected'. In other words, as Coedès has pointed out, Lu Thai was commenting on what he saw as the decline in the influence of the aristocracy based on Hindu cultural tradition, 'made up as it was of the various elements mentioned: nobles, Brahmans, merchants, astrologers and physicians', and was expressing his satisfaction at the trans-valuation of values which had been brought about 'by the break-up of the Indo-Khmer aristocratic society that was so alien to his own Buddhistic ideals' (16:132f).

On the other hand, the Buddhist Thai state had, towards the end of the thirteenth century, established good relations with China. A Chinese diplomat arrived at Sukhodaya in 1282 to negotiate a treaty of friendship between China and the Thais. Twelve years later Rama Kamhaeng himself made a visit to China. He appears to have sufficiently enjoyed his visit to have made a second one six years later, in 1300. He brought back with him on that occasion some Chinese craftsmen, who founded the famous Sawankalok potteries in Thailand. Many of the events of Rama Kamhaeng's reign are known to us from Chinese literary sources, as well as from the stone inscriptions in Thailand (123:54f).

Thirteenth-century Burmese Buddhism

In sharp contrast to the Thais' good relations with China were those of the Burmese during the same period. After their annexation of Yunnan in 1253, the Chinese in 1271 sent a diplomatic mission to the Burmese king of Pagan (in the central Irrawaddy plain), requiring him to pay tribute to Peking. In effect this would have meant that the Burmese king would have become a remote vassal of Kublai Khan. The king of Pagan sent the members of the mission back with expressions of friendly sentiments and nothing more. Two years later another mission, headed by a Chinese ambassador, came to Pagan, with a somewhat threatening message from the great Khan. On the pretext that these diplomats failed to observe Burmese protocol (by keeping their shoes on in the king's presence), the king of Pagan had them executed. Without waiting for Kublai Khan to strike, the Burmese attacked one of China's vassal states which bordered on Burma. The vassal king asked for protection, which Kublai Khan immediately provided, with the result that the Burmese army suffered a severe and damaging defeat. A worsening of relations between China and Burma followed. An invasion of Burma in 1283 led to the eventual Mongol attack on Pagan itself in 1287. The city was occupied briefly by Kublai Khan's grandson, but with no great damage. Earlier writers on Burma's history used to make much of the 'fall of Pagan'. In Harvey's words, Pagan 'perished . . . amid the blood and flame of the Tartar Terror' (30:69). The intensely patriotic Maung Htin Aung tells us that the Tartars sacked the city; that those inhabitants who had not fled – monks, men, women and children – died in the looting and burning; and that temples and monasteries were stripped of their gold and silver, and so on (37:71f). More recent historical scholarship finds, however, that the traumatic nature of the events of 1287 has been greatly exaggerated, and that far from being a great crisis in Burmese history it can be seen in the perspective of a number of political changes, either of capital or of dynasty, which continued down to the nineteenth century; that there 'is no clear evidence of any extensive or widespread damage to the economic structure of society following the Chinese invasions'; and that 'the Theravada religious faith of early thirteenth century Pagan seems to survive without major change throughout the fourteenth and fifteenth centuries' (5:3f). The main effect of the end of the Pagan dynasty was that it enabled the Mons of the south-east, in Martaban and Pegu, to reassert Mon identity, even although this was within the context of general Thai supremacy from Pegu in the west to the Mekong river in the east, and from Chiengrai in the north to the Malay peninsula in the south.

This reassertion of Mon identity, made possible by the decline of Pagan's political power, occurred when a local leader was able to strengthen his control of the area inhabited mainly by Mons from his headquarters at Martaban. His name was Wareru (in Thai he is known as Chao Fa-Rua); his father was Thai and his mother Mon; he was possibly the son-in-law of the king of Sukhodaya, Rama Kamhaeng. Later he succeeded in extending his rule to neighbouring Pegu. His rule gave a new impulse to learning and to a renewal of Buddhism in the whole area surrounding the Gulf of Martaban (16:18f; 7:35). One aspect of the learning which he encouraged is seen in the 'Wareru *dhammathat*', another of the early law codes of Burma, produced under his auspices by Mon monks from old writings, to clear up some of the uncertainty still left by Dhammavilasa's earlier code. Wareru's is a distinctly Indian but non-Brahmanical code, in which the sacerdotal element is disregarded, so that, for example, marriage is not treated as a sacrament (30:111). Wareru's kingdom was nominally a vassal of the Thai Sukhodaya state (from whom he received royal recognition in the shape of a white elephant) but in fact it enjoyed a vigorous independent existence; its people undertook trading overseas and gained a reputation for shipbuilding; one of the major customers for their craft was the Malay kingdom of Malacca (14:60. See also 37:78–80).

At the end of the thirteenth century, therefore, Buddhism was still growing in importance in Burma.

The expansion of Buddhism in Burma

Pagan continued to be a centre of Buddhism well into the fifteenth century (5:17). After what has misleadingly been called the 'fall' of Pagan, monasteries and pagodas continued to be built there. In 1356, for example, a grant of royal land was made for the construction of a monastery; in 1375 a governor of Pagan repaired one pagoda (the Shwezigon) and built another; in 1395 a minister of state of the kingdom of Ava built a new monastery; a queen had a monastery built and visited Pagan for the dedication of it in 1396; another king and his queen built monasteries in 1416 and 1417; a few years later yet another king built a monastery which his son and successor maintained.

Such frequent royal patronage does not mean, however, that Buddhism in Burma even at this time was still the exclusive concern of kings rather than of the people. For monasteries and pagodas, although they were built by kings, existed for the benefit of the lay people. Many of the monks who studied in monastic libraries, engaged in this pursuit not merely for the sake of abstract learning, but for the fuller understanding of the Buddha-Dhamma: of how it applied to human life and how to explain it, and commend it and help men to live by it, whether at the level of ethically fruitful action, or of the analysis and improvement of mental states. Pagodas were for the expression of devotion, where reverence for the Buddha and Buddhahood were fostered, and where in quietness laymen and laywomen could contemplate the peace of which the Buddha taught. In pouring out their wealth on monasteries and pagodas kings were benefiting the people as they would not have done if they had merely used their resources in the aggrandisement of their palaces or in the construction of magnificent tombs and memorials to themselves. Harvey emphasises this aspect of the significance of Pagan's many pagodas and monasteries: 'Vainglorious tyrants build themselves lasting sepulchres, but none of these men [kings of Pagan] has a tomb. It is a mistaken sentiment which contrasts the old-time splendour of Pagan with the mat huts of today. Then as now hut jostled temple and housed even the great; the two were not antithetic but correlative: these men's magnificence was to glorify their religion, not to deck the tent wherein they camped during this transitory life' (30:70).

It was not until after the middle of the fifteenth century that the centre of royal Buddhism shifted finally from Pagan to the new Burmese capitals, Ava and Sagaing, also in the central plain of the Irrawaddy. Coincident with this was a shift of Pali monastic scholarship and learning from Pagan. Scholarly work went on at Pagan until the end of the fourteenth century, however. The Abhidhamma (see Glossary) continued to be a favourite subject of study. Scholars continued to visit Pagan from other Theravada centres; at the end of the fourteenth century the Thai monk-teacher of the king of Chiengmai made the journey to Pagan, and in the early fifteenth century abbots of the chief monastery of Chiengmai studied there. In 1442 a Burmese ruler donated a library of Pali and Sanskrit works to a certain monastery in Pagan which was a notable centre for Abhidhamma study (5:17f).

To the south, in the delta region of Burma, where Pali Buddhism had had a long history among the Mons, the tradition continued uninterrupted. This Pegu region was still open to communication with south India, where Buddhism had maintained itself as a live and growing tradition until at least the twelfth century, as we know, for example, from the important Pali text on Buddhist laymen's ethics called 'The Adornment of the Buddhist Laity' *(Upasaka-janalankara)*, which was composed in the twelfth century by a scholar from south India and was intended for newcomers to the teaching of the Buddha (84:2). This work is known also in Burma. It was natural, therefore, that the Mons around the shores of the Gulf of Martaban, who, as we have seen, were overseas traders and shipbuilders, should have continued to benefit from cultural intercourse with the Buddhists of south India and of Sri Lanka. A particularly notable expedition went from Pegu to that island at the end of the fifteenth century.

Buddhism in the kingdom of Lan-na (Chiengmai)

Thailand in the fourteenth century had not yet become one kingdom extending over the territory which it covers today. By the second half of the century there were four Thai states in the area, including what is now part of Laos. There were (1) Sukhodaya; (2) to the north of it, Lan-na; (3) to the north-east, Lan Chan; and (4) a new kingdom which arose in the middle of the century, in the south of the plain, at Ayudhaya.

In the extreme north was the kingdom of Lan-na ('million rice-fields') with its capital, the newly built city of Chiengmai. Buddhism had been known there for five centuries when Mangrai absorbed a neighbouring Mon state into the kingdom of Lan-na. Mangrai had visited Pagan and had been impressed by Burmese pagoda and monastery architecture. In his own capital of Chiengmai he built a shrine in a style very similar to that of Pagan. Just outside the city he built another, more spectacular, in the style of the Bodh-Gaya temple in India. His reign of fifty years, which lasted until the early fourteenth century (1311), is regarded by modern Thais as notable for the wise administration and the improvement of material conditions, as well as for the spiritual and moral advancement which he effected (20:11).

During the reign of one of Mangrai's successors, a fourteenth-century king named Ku-Na, the Sinhalese tradition and line of ordination, often referred to as the 'Sihala-sasana' (or Sinhalese religion), were introduced into the kingdom of Lan-na. The story is told in detail in the Pali chronicle which was composed in Chiengmai at the beginning of the sixteenth century, the *Jinakalamali* (40). The sequence of events provides a good example of the way the Sihala-sasana spread from one state to another in South-East Asia at that time.

We are told that a certain monk named Sumana was living in Sukhodaya. From there he went down to the city of Ayudhaya, in order to study Buddhist doctrine. The reason for this can be seen in the fact that Ayudhaya was in that part of Thailand which had been the Mon Buddhist kingdom of Dvaravati before it became absorbed into the Khmer empire in the eleventh century. The Buddhist tradition was kept alive there under Khmer rule, and evidently its prestige as a good place for the study of Buddhist doctrine had continued into the fourteenth century. So having spent some time there studying the doctrine, Sumana returned to the Thai capital at Sukhodaya. We are no doubt to understand from this note about his visit to Ayudhaya that he was a serious and scholarly monk. What we are told next in the course of the story enables us to draw the further conclusion that even the Mon tradition, as it existed then in Thailand, was regarded as somewhat deficient by Sinhalese standards. For Sumana, back in

Sukhodaya, heard that a great sage by the name of Udambara had come from Sri Lanka to the Mon country of lower Burma. No sooner did he hear this than he set off with a companion to visit the sage from Sri Lanka. Not only were they able to improve their understanding of Buddhist doctrines by attending on this renowned Sinhalese monk, but also they received from him re-ordination in the Sinhalese tradition, that is the tradition of the Maha Vihara, the Great Monastery in Sri Lanka, ordination which had originally been received from India long ago in Asoka's time.

Evidently, the Sinhalese sage's fame had spread far, for he received an envoy from Lu Thai, the king of Sukhodaya, requesting him to provide 'a monk who was competent to perform all the acts of the Order'. He thereupon dispatched the Elder Sumana, 'in order that he might perform all the acts of the Order in the city of Sukhodaya' (41:84).

The king of Sukhodaya, we are told, overjoyed at his good fortune in getting such a treasure of a monk, had a new monastery built; this was the Ambavana (or Mango Grove) Vihara, (now known as Wat Pa Ma-muang, to the east of the city). Thus, 'true' Sinhalese ordination was brought first to lower Burma, and then from lower Burma to the Thai kingdom of Sukhodaya in the fourteenth century. Soon after this it appears that an ancient 'relic', said to have been deposited in Sukhodaya long before, in Asoka of India's time, became aroused, so to speak, and performed a miracle. The relic itself lay hidden, but a Brahman came by night and let Sumana into the secret of where it was hidden. This Brahman who came by night was, according to the chronicle, really a tree-deity in disguise. The relic was then excavated and given an exposition before the king, who worshipped it with due reverence. But the relic, it seems, did not wish to stay in the city of Sukhodaya, and indicated as much to the king by performing another miracle.

It so happened that at about that time another king, Ku-Na of Chiengmai, was also feeling anxious to have a monk who was fully ordained according to the Sinhalese tradition and who could perform all the necessary rites and so on. He, too, sent a request to the Sinhalese sage Udambara down in lower Burma for just such a man. The monk who then came to Chiengmai in response to this request turned out, however, to be not quite entirely satisfactory; he had some doubts, apparently, about ordaining some of the forest-dwelling monks. Eventually Sumana was sent from Sukhodaya to Chiengmai. With him came his wonderful relic, which had not wished to stay in Sukhodaya, and which performed miracles 'of utmost wonder' at every stop on the journey, no doubt signifying its approval of the move (41:86). The historically important theme in all this is evidently the onward progress of Sinhalese Buddhism from Sri Lanka to Chiengmai.

In the kingdom of Lan-na the Sinhalese tradition became firmly rooted. There was 'a resurgence of zeal and devotion', shown by the number of Wats built in Chiengmai and Lampun at this time (20:11). There was an increase, too, in the energy and effort devoted to Buddhist Pali scholarship. Notable especially were the works of religious history, such as the *Jinakalamali*, witten in Pali at Chiengmai, from whose pages we have just had one or two glimpses of this period. Commentarial works were also written there, and a life of the Buddha, entitled *Pathamasambodhi*.

The rise of Ayudhaya : Khmer culture and Thai Buddhism

The kingdom of Sukhodaya, founded early in the thirteenth century, was not destined to enjoy independence for long. It had flourished under the rule of Rama Kamhaeng as a well integrated Buddhist state, but only until about the end of the fourteenth century. For Rama Kamhaeng died in 1317, and after him there were only three successors as kings of an independent Sukhodaya. During their reigns the Buddhist tradition which their great predecessor had established was maintained. The second of them, named Lu Thai (1357–76), was so renowned a scholar and patron of Buddhism that he came to be known as Maha Dhammaraja (Great Righteous King). He devoted himself to the organisation of the Sangha, distinguishing between the Aranyavasi (or forest-dwelling) monks and the Gamavasis (or town-dwellers). The former appear to have lived in seclusion in forest areas for the purpose of practising meditation; the latter were concerned mainly with the study of the Pali scriptures and their town monasteries were centres for the study of the various scriptures and doctrines. King Lu Thai himself became a monk for a time, and established the custom which Thai laymen have followed since that time, of spending a few months living the life of a monk, often the four months of the rainy season, the so-called Buddhist 'Lent'. King Lu Thai was a scholar, and composed a treatise on Buddhist cosmology, entitled *Trai-bhumi-katha*, 'An Account of the Three Worlds' – that is heaven, earth and hell. He also devoted time to getting monasteries built, and roads also, in order to make travel and communication easier, both for monks and the ordinary people. Buddhist monks are often well travelled; they certainly do not live in stagnating seclusion, but travel about from monastery to monastery and from village to village, meeting other monks and lay people and discussing and exchanging ideas. The making of Buddha statues was also highly developed during the later Sukhodaya period of Thailand's history.

During Lu Thai's reign, however, a new and rival power had been growing in the southern part of the Menam plain. This was the kingdom of Ayudhaya, founded in the reign preceding Lu Thai's, in the year 1350. Initially, this new kingdom exhibited a rather different spirit from that of Sukhodaya. For illustration of this point it is useful to refer to what Coedès tells us about how Lu Thai tried to govern. According to an inscription which he himself put up:

> This king rules by observing the ten kingly precepts. He has pity on all his subjects. If he sees rice belonging to others, he does not covet it, and if he sees the wealth of others he does not become indignant . . . He has never beaten to death someone who has done wrong, whatever the crime may have been. Whenever he has captured warriors or enemy combatants, he has neither killed them nor had them beaten, but has kept them and fed them so as to preserve them from ruin and destruction . . . The reason why he represses his feelings and curbs his thoughts, and refrains from anger when anger is called for, is that he desires to become a Buddha and to lead all creatures beyond the sea of suffering of transmigration.

This may or may not always have been entirely fulfilled, but it expresses what the king believed to be the correct policy to be followed. It is, as Coedès comments, in striking contrast to the spirit and methods of Hindu Khmer rule, as this is set out in Cambodian epigraphy; the two codes 'differ on almost every point' (16:145).

It was the Khmer traditions that appear to have been revived in the new kingdom of Ayudhaya. The emergence of this new centre of political power in the southern part of the Menam plain represented, so far as trends in government and ideas were concerned, a contrast with what had happened in the north. The area in which the new kingdom arose was one in which Khmer political power and culture had been strong, although the latter had been modified by the Buddhism of the Mons to some extent. This influence seems to have been felt more in the realm of art and culture, however, than in that of ideas. The same seems to have been true of the new kingdom of Ayudhaya, which was Buddhist in some respects, for it remained a centre for Buddhist scholarship and literature; this was not true, however, so far as its law codes and its social organisation were concerned. These were revivals of the old Hindu Khmer code, harsh and repressive; all of them were non-Buddhist texts, composed or inspired by Brahmans who inherited the traditions of Angkor (16:147).

Ayudhaya, in the southern part of the Menam plain, was only a small town and trading centre before it began to emerge as a centre of political power under the man who subsequently became known as King Ramatibodi I. Nothing is known for certain about this man's ancestry; he may have been of Mon origin, he may have been Khmer. He had previously become ruler of a place called Utong, to the west of Ayudhaya, an achievement made possible partly by marrying the previous ruler's daughter. In 1350 he made Ayudhaya his capital, as it was better situated for controlling his expanding territories. His government very quickly took the form of an absolute monarchy on Khmer lines. The king was an autocrat, virtually a god-king, although in this case the theory was somewhat modified, to the extent that he was regarded as a 'living Buddha' rather than a Hindu god-king. The northern Thai kingdom of Sukhodaya eventually succumbed to this growing power of Ayudhaya. This happened at last in the year 1378, after a seven year period of fairly successful resistance to the expansionist policy of Ayudhaya's second king, Boromaraja I. The kingdom of Sukhodaya thus lasted only 140 years, but during that relatively short time it had made significant and memorable contributions to the development of Thai Buddhism. For a further sixty years it continued as a vassal state under the control of Ayudhaya until 1438, when it was completely absorbed into the Ayudhayan empire, and Sukhodaya gradually became a provincial town, preserving only some visible evidence of the once flourishing Buddhist capital it had been.

2

Consequences of Contact with Europe

Early European contacts with Thailand and Burma

When Europeans first made their presence felt in Thailand, at the beginning of the sixteenth century, the royal capital was at Ayudhaya. This was a city built on an island in the Menam river, some forty miles north of the modern capital, Bangkok; by name at least, Ayudhaya is well known nowadays to tourists in Thailand on account of the many medieval buildings and ruins which are still to be seen there. In its day, which lasted from the middle of the fourteenth century to its destruction by the Burmese in 1767, it was a magnificent city reflecting in many ways the splendour of the Khmer cities and civilisation of Cambodia. There were numerous wats, or monasteries, many of royal foundation, magnificent today even as ruins. One of these is the royal Wat Buddhaisvarya, on the left bank of the river; another, particularly elaborate, on the right bank of the river, is said to have been inspired by the style of the great shrines of the Khmer empire (20:17). Throughout the history of the Ayudhayan kingdom the royal building of monasteries and other acts of merit continued. In the earlier period King Boroma Trailokanath (1448–88) was particularly zealous in this respect. His long reign was one of the most important periods in Ayudhaya's history, a time of consolidation of the empire which the earlier Ayudhayan kings had won. King Boroma was keenly interested in the affairs of the Sangha and devoted much of his time to the task of rationalising its administration. He himself was ordained as a monk for a time and lived the monastic life, achieving fame for his scholarship. In one respect, however, the Ayudhayan empire shrank a little during his time, owing to the loss of part of the extreme south, namely Malacca. A former Mahayana Buddhist ruler of that region, Paramesvara, having been exiled at the beginning of the fifteenth century, returned to Malacca as governor, having changed his religion from Buddhist to Muslim, and his name to Megat Iskander Shah. As governor of Malacca he acknowledged the king of Ayudhaya as his overlord. But during King Boroma Trailokanath's reign, in 1455, some Arab merchants in Malacca instigated a rebellion against Thai rule, a rebellion which was put down at the time, but soon broke out again, this time successfully, with the result that Malacca became an independent Muslim kingdom (99:41).

Islam had thus appeared on the Thai horizon, and the Muslim minority among the people of southern Thailand eventually developed as the base of the one non-Buddhist religious community of any size in the country. Islam, however, did not have the proselytising success it was having elsewhere in South–East Asia at this time, although of the three major Semitic-Greek religions, Judaism, Christianity and Islam, it was Islam which had slightly more missionary success in Thailand than had Christianity.

In Burma it was to the city and port of Pegu, on the eastern edge of the Irrawaddy delta, that the first Europeans, the Portuguese, came in the early part of the sixteenth century. Pegu was one of the centres of the Mon people, who occupied most of the delta region of lower Burma. Because of an early connection with the Telangana coast in south India they were also known in Burma as 'Talaings'. There is a long-standing tradition of conflict between the Mons in the south and the Burmese, who at that time occupied mainly the central and northern parts of what is now known as Burma. When the Portuguese first came to the south-east coast of Burma, in 1511, there had been a period of about forty years of peace and prosperity in Pegu. It had begun in the time of Dhammaceti, a Mon king who had formerly been a Buddhist monk. As a young man he had helped a Mon princess named Shinsawbu to escape from Ava. She had been taken there by the Burmese king Thihathu, following a campaign he made into Mon territory in lower Burma. At Ava she was kept in virtual captivity, and so devoted herself to religious study and practice. She had with her as tutors two monks from her own country, and with their help she escaped from the palace, went aboard a small boat with the monks, and came down the river, eventually to Pegu. Years later, in 1453, she succeeded to the throne of Pegu at the death of her father, Binnyakyan (who is remembered for having increased the height of the spire of the Shwe Dagon pagoda in Rangoon to 302 feet). As queen of Pegu she was greatly loved by the Mon people, so that in the nineteenth century the highest compliment their descendants in lower Burma could find to bestow on Queen Victoria was 'Queen Shinsawbu reincarnated'. Her reign was a time of unusual peace. She retired from public affairs in 1460 and one of the two monks who had helped her to escape Dhammaceti was nominated as regent in her place. He left the Sangha and married the queen's daughter, eventually succeeding to the throne of Pegu at the death of Queen Shinsawbu in 1472. The queen had spent her years of retirement at Rangoon, and had once again devoted herself to religious matters; one of her works was the enlargement of the Shwe Dagon pagoda by the addition of a terrace 'fifty feet high, three hundred yards wide, with a great stone balustrade, a circle of stone lamps and several encircling walls between which she planted palm trees . . . When her end came at the age of seventy-eight she had her bed placed where she could see the Shwe Dagon, and thus, with her eyes fixed on that wondrous spire, she breathed her last' (30: 95, 97 and 117f; 37: 93 and 98–100).

The Mon kingdom in lower Burma had the ex-monk Dhammaceti as king for the next twenty years, from 1472 to 1492. As ruler of Pegu he was famous for his statesmanship and renowned for his piety (8:37). As king he had the power to carry into effect what as monk he had already seen to be desirable, namely the re-ordering of the Sangha. In 1475 he sent a mission of twenty-two monks to Sri Lanka, bearing many gifts for the Temple of the Tooth, for the leading monks, and for the king of Sri Lanka. The object of their visit was to take ordination again in the ancient Sinhalese order, the reputation of which was at that time very high throughout the Theravada countries of Asia; the sacred shrines of Sri Lanka, too, 'were regarded almost with the same veneration as those in the Holy Land of Buddhism' (70: 330). Having received Sinhalese ordination at a ceremony at Kalaniya, near Colombo, they returned to Pegu and were able to re-ordain Buddhist monks throughout Burma into the Sinhalese line, thus providing for several of the sects into which the monks of Burma had been divided the opportunity of becoming united again. A record of the events was inscribed on ten stones, known as the Kalyani inscriptions; these constitute the major source of our knowledge of King Dhammaceti's reform, as well as for a good deal of earlier

24

Mon history. The place of the ordinations in Pegu was known as the Kalyani-*sima*, or 'ordination-enclosure', and it was there that the inscriptions were set up. Monks from all over lower Burma, from Ava and Toungoo, from the Shan kingdoms, from Thailand and Cambodia were able to come and receive this ancient ordination, which gave them a link with Mahinda, the founder of the Sangha in Sri Lanka in the third century BC.

During Dhammaceti's reign lower Burma had a long period of peace. The king commissioned one of the most learned of the monks to translate a Peguan law code (the law code of Wareru) into Burmese, so that it might be used in the Burmese kingdom of Ava also. He himself, apparently, made no distinction between Mons and Burmese; 'the two races were tied to each other by the silken bonds of a common religion and a common heritage' (37:101).

Thus it was that lower Burma had enjoyed an unusually long period of peace by the time the Portuguese arrived in the Gulf of Martaban. The sea route from Europe was discovered in 1498, and soon Portuguese ships began to find their way to the shores of India and South–East Asia. By 1511 the first Portuguese had arrived at Pegu.

Although in the north of Burma Shan and Burmese had plenty of battles to keep them busy, in Pegu conditions were settled, the rulers were mild-tempered, and it was something like a golden age, according to G. E. Harvey (30:121). 'The King of Pegu', wrote an Italian merchant in 1515, 'is so humane and domestic that an infant might speak to him' (30:121). Pegu had considerable trade of the kind which attracted the Portuguese: besides rubies and gems from upper Burma, lac, wax, ivory, horn, lead, tin, and other goods from the interior, there were also the products of Sumatra, Borneo, and China, brought by sea: pepper, camphor and porcelain.

Into this prosperous kingdom in the early sixteenth century came the Portuguese, some as traders, some as merchant adventurers, some as mercenaries ready to join in any fray where the prospects of booty were good, some as roving companies hard to distinguish from bandits (see 30:153ff).

It was at this time that the Burmese, in retreat from a Shan invasion of the plains of upper Burma, had found a stronghold at Toungoo in the Sittang valley, between the Shan hill-country in the north and Pegu in the south. By 1535, having been pent up there for long enough, they began to make forays into the Mon area, attracted, like the Portuguese, by the prospect of loot. They attacked Pegu, Prome, and Martaban, sometimes aided by Portuguese adventurers such as Joano Cayeyro and his merry men, who had muskets and light artillery to contribute. The Mon city of Martaban was their richest prize, where, as spoils awaiting the victor, stood the warehouses of merchants of many nationalities: Portuguese, Greek, Venetian, Moorish, Jewish, Armenian, Persian, Abyssinian, Malabari Indian, and Sumatran, according to Harvey. The sack of this city lasted for three days. 'The palace and town were burnt to the ground. The captive prince with all his family and followers, men and women, were cruelly exterminated in spite of a promise of good treatment. Scores of nobles were flung into the river with stones round their necks, and the remaining property of the merchants, mostly foreigners, was confiscated' (30:157).

It is possible to see the campaigns of the Burmese as having the extension of Burmese power as their ultimate aim. The immediate result, however, was to breed further violence among their own ranks. Bayin Naung, the Burmese leader, was later compelled to reconquer from his own relatives, and with the aid of the Portuguese De Mello and his men, territory which had only recently been unified under Burmese rule. Whereas in the eleventh century the Burmese kings of Pagan had evolved a great and distinctive Buddhist civilisation at Pagan, the later Burmese of the Toungoo and Shwebo dynasties 'seem to have spent all their energies in trying to unite a divided country and in embarking on military adventures and territorial expansion', comments Coedès (16:190).

Nevertheless Bayin Naung (king of Toungoo 1551–81) considered himself a great Buddhist king. He acted, in his own eyes at least, as the champion of Theravada Buddhism throughout the South–East Asian mainland. He had temples and monasteries built wherever his campaigns of conquest took him, and made ceremonial visits to the old Burmese capital at Pagan in central Burma and donated a large bronze bell to the Shwezigon pagoda, engraved with an account of all his victories. He tried to stamp out the Nat cult, issuing edict after edict against it (23:67). In his public promotion of Buddhism he was trying, observes Maung Htin Aung, to make sure that what was happening in Ceylon, namely the infiltration of Portuguese political power as a by-product of Catholic conversion, including even the conversion of a Sinhalese king, did not happen in Burma (37:123ff).

The role of the Buddhist Sangha in all this was not easy. On the career of Bayin Naung, Sarkisyanz observes that 'Costly offerings to pagodas may have been this monarch's attempt to atone for his power struggles of blood and iron' (86:7). Or they may have been the expression of what he conceived to be his religious duty. It often became necessary for the Buddhist monks to intervene and exert upon kings and rulers the influence which theoretically the teaching of the Buddha expected to have in a Buddhist state. They 'tried to temper violence against dynastic rivals', or to reproach fratricidal kings. 'Rajadirit (Yazadirit) of the Shan dynasty ruling class was (in 1401) persuaded to recall his forces approaching the Burmese capital Ava, when a monk sent by his adversary explained to him the implications of destroying human life as a great obstacle to rebirth as a human being' (that is, he was liable to be reborn in some much lower, less desirable state of being (hell, for example, or, if not that, as a wild animal of some sort). So too in the sixteenth century the monks were active in similar ways, as, for example, 'when a military setback induced the Burmese conqueror king Bayin Naung to "lock up into heat . . . in order to burn to death" his defeated commander and his men, "the totality of Burmese, Mon and outside abbots exaltedly deigned to unite, (and) extinguishing the fire, they released the lord and the totality of his soldiers from the heat", escorting them into the safety of their monasteries' (86:76). Again and again, observes Sarkisyanz, the Buddhist monks engaged in their traditional role of saving lives from despots and penal laws (86:76).

Portuguese ambitions to establish a Portuguese Catholic colony in Burma were demonstrated in the support from Goa, the colony in India, for Philip de Brito, an adventurer who about the year 1600 succeeded in getting himself proclaimed king of Syriam (a small town in Burma across the river from Rangoon). The Buddhist monks' principles must have been severely strained in this case, for de Brito had gone far beyond the misdemeanours of Burmese kings: he had converted (through his Jesuit chaplains) the Mon inhabitants of his 'kingdom' to Roman Catholicism and then, with the approval of the ecclesiastical hierarchy of Goa, in the interests of suppressing idolatry, he had stripped Buddhist temples of their treasures, destroyed pagodas, melted down the gold, and turned monastery bells into gun metal, accumulating for himself in the process a fortune in gold coins (30:186). He was, comments Harvey, 'a sample of the heroic scoundrels who built up Portuguese dominion in the East, was unscrupulous like the princes against whom he was pitted' (30:188f). His 'Kingdom' was eventually, in 1613, reconquered by the Burmese king Nanda Bayin and de Brito put to death by impalement. Six years later a portentous event for Burma occurred: the English East India Company was granted the right to set up a factory at Syriam. Not long after this, in 1635, the Burmese kings, who had until then been using Pegu as their capital, withdrew to Ava in the Irrawaddy plain of central Burma, and there, in their more remote inland city, 'became shut off from foreign influence and remained in dangerous ignorance about what was going on in the world' (16:185), in distinct contrast to the Thai kings, both of Ayudhaya and later of Bangkok.

On the one hand, we see throughout the sixteenth and seventeenth centuries in Burma the violence of the Burmese kings, notably represented by the megalomaniac Bayin Naung (15:191), and their opportunist Portuguese accomplices, or sometimes, protagonists. It was a curious and contradictory partnership. For the Burmese it was a religiously meritorious deed to build a pagoda; for the Portuguese it was a religiously meritorious deed to knock one down. For the Portuguese, Catholic loyalty meant opposition to Buddhism and the despoiling of Buddhist shrines; for the Burmese kings of this period it meant making amends for their misdeeds by lavish donations from the spoils of their 'unifying' wars; wars which were unifying in intention but so often turned out to be divisive, with the result that, in 1599, Burma had practically lost all political cohesion (15:193). On the other hand there were the monks, attempting, often, to maintain their traditional role as the preservers of Buddhist values, sometimes succeeding, sometimes not, and themselves suffering as a consequence of the violence of the times. Towards the close of the sixteenth century, when the Burmese King Nanda Bayin was making a series of attacks on Thailand, conscription of young men for the army was introduced. Mons and Burmese alike resented this and many entered the monkhood to escape. In retaliation, Nanda Bayin, on the pretext of reforming the Sangha, forced many monks to become laymen. Many of the abbots of monasteries, with whom alone rests the right to give or withhold ordination, publicly expressed the hope that these knavish tricks might be ended by Nanda Bayin's speedy downfall. The king replied to this by sending many such abbots into exile into upper Burma.

The Theravada states: kings and cults

If there was a discernible pattern to the aggressive warlord policy followed by the Burmese kings Bayin Naung and Nanda Bayin during the second half of the sixteenth century it was opposition to the Thais, wherever they were to be found, whether in the Shan States of Burma, in Lan Chang (Laos), or Lan-na (Chiengmai) or in Ayudhaya. Yet all these kings were Buddhists; the most warlike of all, Bayin Naung evidently saw himself, as Hall puts it, 'as a model Buddhist King, building pagodas where ever he went, distributing copies of the Pali scriptures, feeding monks, and promoting the collection and study of the dhammathats' (law books) (27:296). Not content with these deeds of Buddhist merit, he took the further step of sending offerings to the renowned relic shrine in Sri Lanka, the Temple of the Sacred Tooth (the Tooth referred to was, so it was alleged, that of Gautama the Buddha). There is a coherence between these two facts, that the most aggressive nation builder was also the most devout and energetic Buddhist, and it is this: that Theravada Buddhism often attracted the kings of South–East Asia for its socially and culturally cohesive qualities just as much as Theravada monks were often attracted to kings as protectors and propagators of the Theravada religion. This arrangement is a system character- istic of Buddhist South–East Asia: the king, as the patrimonial leader of his people, must combine *morality* with his *power*. For the people of his realm must have a sense of a supporting system of morality in terms of which the king's power is exercised; otherwise he becomes a tyrant, and they rebel. Since so many South–East Asian rulers – Burmese, Thai, and Lao – had come to the fore by means of a pragmatic struggle for power, they had also to spend time demonstrating their morality and convincing the general populace that they were rulers who upheld the moral system and had the ability and the intention of providing material benefits to morally worthy subjects. 'At the apex of the political pyramid stands the very moral symbol and moral protector of the society, traditionally the king, with the wheel of morality as his symbol' (39:32). It was this which differentiated Buddhist kingship in South–East Asia from Hindu kingship. In the Hindu case the king is a god incarnate, and that constitutes his authority and provides him with his sanctions. In the Buddhist case the king is a man, whose authority rests in his pragmatic achieve- ment of power, *supported* by his loyal adherence to a universally (throughout the state) accepted system of morality, namely Theravada Buddhism. As Heine-Geldern has put it: 'Where Hinduism prevailed the king was considered to be either an incarnation of a god or a descendant of a god, or both. Mostly it was Siva who was thought to incarnate himself in kings or to engender dynasties . . . The theory of divine incarnation as found in Hinduism and Mahayana is incompatible with the doctrine of the Buddhism of the Hinayana' (34:7). This difference, the same writer goes on to point out, expresses itself even in the layout of the respective capital cities. In the Khmer Shaivite capital the temple of the god was at the centre of the city – the sacred, cosmic centre: Mount Meru. It is the 'central mountain' (at the heart of the cosmos in Hindu tradition) inhabited by the Lord of the universe. Since Theravada Buddhism does not give central place to a supreme deity there will not normally be a temple for a supreme deity, certainly not at the centre of the capital city. Nevertheless, enough of the Mahayana and Hindu conception of kingship had survived in Burma for the king to be regarded, in practice, as 'Indra', the ruler of the universe, (and, in particular, of this part of it called Burma) and therefore his *palace* must be, by implication, the Burmese state's 'Mount Meru'.

There was evidently a tension between these two concepts of royalty which once existed in Buddhist South–East Asia. Some kings seem to have adhered somewhat more to the concept of moral sanction while others adhered more to the concept of divine sanction. Where it was the former, the king would tend to pay more regard, outwardly at least, to the accepted system of morality, the Buddhist religion, and its representatives and upholders, the Sangha. 'This religion of the supreme Buddha endures under the patronage of kings,' wrote the nineteenth-century Burmese monk Pannasami (88:152).

The other side of this fact is that the peoples of the Buddhist states of South–East Asia see Buddhism as a system of morality, not as an ideology. Ideas of all kinds are to be welcomed and given hospitality within the cultural system; what is resisted and rejected is any tendency at dogmatic teaching which would lead to attempts to change or disrupt the traditional system of morality which provides the *social* cohesion. Such resistance was met by Christian and Islamic missionaries, whenever they went beyond the bounds of hospitality and tried to push their ideologies to the logical extreme by attempting to found new, alternative moralities, resulting in the emergence of socially disruptive new communities.

This hospitality to *ideas* of all kinds, so long as they were not tied to invasive ideologies, was observed by the sixteenth-century Portuguese traveller Fernao Mendez Pinto, who in 1554 put into writing an account of his recent experiences in Pegu, Ayudhaya, Malacca, and Japan. The Thais, he observed, were a nation of believers in many strange gods and spirits. There was, for example, a large idol with ever-open jaws and a banquet table spread in front of it; the idol was served by fifty old women who called this strange deity by the honourable name of 'the god of the enlargement of the stomach'. People worship also the spirits of the waters, of fire, and of the earth. The king 'interferes with nobody's religious beliefs, for he claims to be only the master of men's bodies, not their souls' (48:534). There is an interesting parallel here to the Thai king's English contemporary, Queen Elizabeth I, who is said to have claimed that she wished 'to make windows into no man's soul' (Chakrapat of Ayudhaya, 1549–65; Elizabeth I of England 1558–1603). At the eclipse of the moon, believed by the Thai people to be a snake attempting to swallow the moon, they 'shoot at the sky, pound on the gates of their houses, and yell at it from both land and water' in order to force the snake to give up its prey (48:534). Just as such spirit worship and folk cults remained the staple elements of the popular culture of Thailand, so also, as we have seen, have they remained within that of Burma, in the form of the Nat cult, and also in alchemy and astrology (35:1–5). Occasionally an over-zealous Buddhist king such as Bayin Naung would try to stamp out the spirit cult. But it is clear that in general the continuance of all kinds of indigenous popular beliefs and practices did not detract from the support given to the monks by both rulers and the people of Buddhist South–East Asia. In 1587 Ralph Fitch arrived in Burma, apparently the first Englishman to have done so. He, too, wrote an account of his travels, which includes a frequently quoted reference to the Shwe Dagon pagoda at Rangoon, which, he says, 'is of wonderfull bignesse, and all gilded from the foot to the toppe. It is the fairest place, as I suppose, that is in the world.' What is equally interesting, and possibly more significant as a testimony to the position held by Buddhist monks in Burmese society in the sixteenth century, is his description of the members of the Sangha, whom he calls the 'Tallipoies' (from Talapoins):

The Tallipoies go very strangely apparelled with one camboline or thinne cloth next to their body of a brown colour, another of yellow doubled many times upon their shoulder: and those two be girded to them with a broad girdle; and they have a skinne of leather hanging on a string about their necks, whereupon they sit, bareheaded and barefooted: for none of them weareth shoes; with their right armes bare and a great broad sombrero or shadow in their hand to defend them in the Summer from the Sunne, and in the Winter from the rain. They keepe their feasts by the Moone: and when it is new Moone they keepe their greatest feasts: and then the people send rice and other things to that kiack or church of which they be; and there all the Tallipoies doe meete which be of that Churche, and eate the victuals which are sent them. When the Tallipoies do preach, many of the people carry them gifts into the pulpit where they sit and preach. And there is one that sitteth by them to take that which the people bring. It is divided among them. They have none other ceremonies nor service that I could see, but onely preaching (27:274).

Fitch's observations, which are those of an outsider, are accurate in principle, though not entirely so in point of detail, for the members of the Sangha did perform other ceremonies, such as the fortnightly Uposatha and daily chanting of Suttas, for instance. But the emphasis is correctly made: the ceremonies of Theravada Buddhism, such as they are, are almost entirely verbal. The chanting of verses, rules, formulae, and ascriptions of praise provide one of the main items of diet; the other is the exposition of some passage of the Pali scriptures by a monk, to which the people listen with varying degrees of attention, for the value of hearing Buddhist sermons lies not necessarily in absorbing the sense of what is said; even the very act of hearing a sermon is a source of merit. Apart from such activities Pali Buddhism has no *corporate* rituals of a sacramental kind, in which the members of the Sangha administer holy things to the people; they are, rather, like Protestant pastors, first and foremost and all the time ministers of the *word*. But in popular Buddhist practice there is a place for cultic rituals elsewhere.

Another interesting resemblance to the left wing of Protestantism is the congregational principle of organisation which characterises *village* Buddhism in South–East Asia, even although under another aspect Buddhism was an institution encouraged and promoted by kings. The people of a village supported the monks as they existed as a local group living in the village monastery. Each local congregation of monks was independent of any external, superior authority. Although in Thailand from the time of the Bangkok dynasty onwards a kind of ecclesiastical hierarchy developed, with royal encouragement, at the end of the seventeenth century, in Thailand as elsewhere the local congregation of monks was subject only to the head of the monastery, who enjoyed freedom of jurisdiction even although he would, as a village abbot, give respect to the abbot of a royal monastery, that is one endowed and supported by the king. The abbots of these royal monasteries were, understandably, called royal abbots or *Sangharajas :* in Thai, sancrats. Their special status is mentioned in the account given by a French writer of the seventeenth century, de La Loubère:

> Every convent is under the conduct of a superior called Chaou-Wat [the 'Personage' of the Wat] that is to say, Lord or Master of the Convent; but all the Superiors are not of equal dignity: the most honourable are those which they call Sancrat, and Sancrat of the Convent of the Palace is the most reverend of all. Yet *no* superior, nor no Sancrat has authority or jurisdiction over another. The missionaries have compared the Sancrats to our bishops . . . [for] none but the Sancrats indeed can make talapoins [fully ordained monks] as none but bishops can make priests. But otherwise the Sancrats have not any jurisdiction nor any authority, neither over the people, nor over the talapoins which are not of their convent; and they could not inform me whether they have any particular character which makes them Sancrats, save that they are superiors of certain convents designed for Sancrats . . .

By Sancrats is meant, de La Loubère makes clear, those monks to whom the king gives 'a name, an umbrella, a sedan, and some men to carry it; but the Sancrats do not make use of this equipage, only to wait upon the king . . .'.

The presence of the French in seventeenth-century Thailand is part of the larger story of the coming of the European powers to South–East Asia, which began in the sixteenth century. In the seventeenth century they began to arrive in larger numbers, not only Portuguese but English, Dutch, Greeks and French. In the long term this connection with Europe had important effects on Buddhism in South–East Asia, and to the beginnings of this in the seventeenth century we must now turn our attention.

Thailand remains Thai and Buddhist

The Portuguese were joined in Thailand by the Dutch and the English during the first two decades of the seventeenth century. In each case it was as merchants that they came, to establish themselves and if possible to eliminate their rivals. The Dutch persuaded the Thai king that they were a much superior nation to the Portuguese, as, among other things, they had invented the telescope and were thus able to observe their enemies without themselves being observed. English merchants arrived in Ayudhaya for the first time in August 1612, on a vessel named 'Globe', small enough to sail up the Menam river to the inland port which was also the capital, where they could unload their cargo and start trading.

The king in Ayudhaya at this time was Song Tham (1610–28), 'the prince who observes the Law' (i.e. the Dhamma). He, too, before becoming king had been a Buddhist monk. He is said to have been a great scholar and devoted to the Buddhist way of life. He was of more peaceful disposition than some kings of Ayudhaya and cultivated good relations not only with various European nations but also with the Shogun of Japan. His name is particularly venerated in Thailand on account of the discovery of a huge 'footprint' of the Buddha in the province of Sarabari during his reign. According to the accepted story, the matter started when a group of monks went from Thailand to Sri Lanka during the early years of his reign to worship at Sumanakuta, the shrine of the Buddha's footprint on a mountain top, known also as 'Adam's Peak', so called because early Muslim travellers believed that Sri Lanka had been the original Paradise from which Adam had been banished, and that the giant primogenitor of the human race had left his footprint on the mountain top. The 'footprint' thus attracted Muslim pilgrims from the ninth century, although it had already been identified by Buddhists as the Buddha's footprint: 'the Master rose, and left the trace of his footprint plain to sight on Sumanakuta' (58:I, 77). However, when the pilgrim-monks from Thailand reached the island of Sri Lanka to do homage at this famous spot they were asked by the Sinhalese monks why they had taken the trouble to make such a journey when they had *five* such 'footprints' in Thailand. They hurried back to Ayudhaya to tell the king this news, and the king ordered that a search should be made for any sign of such sacred places. Eventually, so the story says, a hunter in pursuit of a deer he had wounded saw it struggle, exhausted and near dead, into a thicket. A moment later, it emerged totally recovered, and darted away. The hunter entered the thicket to find the explanation and saw a large footprint in the rock, about a metre long, and containing water. Concluding that the water must have miraculous powers he applied it to the eczema on his own body, from which he had suffered for a long time, and immediately it was cured. The hunter's story was reported to the king, who hurried out to see for himself. The king became convinced that this must indeed be one of the Buddha's footprints mentioned by the Sinhalese monks (57:59f).

It was this king, Song Tham, who in 1623 had a shrine built over the footprint in the rock, and inaugurated with extensive celebrations an annual pilgrimage to the Buddha Footprint.

Relations with European countries were developed in the second half of the century under another famous king of Ayudhaya, Narai the Great (1656–88). The English dropped out of the picture for a while, largely owing to the difficulties which the East India Company made for itself in Thailand by its policies. The French were most in favour. A French Catholic mission had been established, and was recognised by the Pope in 1659. The headquarters of the mission was set up in Ayudhaya, where, it seemed, 'the general atmosphere was agreeable to religious propaganda . . . and religious toleration prevailed among the people' (99:80). King Narai showed himself friendly and made gifts of land and houses. Such generosity caused the French bishops and priests to think he was about to become a Christian, but as in other such cases they were disappointed. The king was not a particularly zealous Buddhist but he was a Buddhist and intended to stay one. He was similarly unresponsive to the proselytising activities of Muslim missionaries from Sumatra, who arrived in Thailand in 1668 and tried to convert him to Islam. Relations with the French remained good, however, and for a while Thailand had as one of its highest government officials a Catholic by the name of Phaulkon, a Greek adventurer who had by his own ingenuity, cleverness, and energy won himself a place as an officer of state and a naturalised Thai nobleman. In Ayudhaya he married a Catholic girl of Japanese family, and under the influence of the French priests was converted to Catholicism. He was intimate with the Jesuit missionaries as well as with King Narai, and it was this which no doubt helped to create the impression in the mind of the Pope and of Louis XIV of France that Thailand was a great mission field full of splendid promise. But success breeds envy, and Phaulkon's case was no exception. Thai officials began to resent his position and to fear that Thailand would be brought entirely under French Catholic domination. The heir to the throne of Ayudhaya was an adopted son of King Narai (he had no natural heir) and Phaulkon had succeeded in converting this young man to Catholicism, so it was alleged. Early in 1688, when the king became seriously ill and about to die, two prominent officers of the Guards arrested Phaulkon on a charge of treason, had him beheaded and the young heir killed, and thus ensured that Thailand remained Thai and Buddhist.

A seventeenth-century English account of Thai Buddhism

From the early seventeenth century, English accounts of Buddhist life and practice in Thailand begin to appear. One such, by a man named Purchas, presents a coherent and convincing picture, although when he comes to deal with Thai Buddhist beliefs he is less convincing.

The Thai people have among them many religious men, observes Purchas. They lead an austere life and have a great reputation for holiness. 'They live in common; they may not marry, nor speak to a woman (which fault is punished with death).' This is not in fact what the Pali code of discipline for Buddhist monks, the Patimokkha, provides. The four most serious offences named there are sexual misconduct, theft, murder and boasting of the power to perform miracles. For these four offences the penalty prescribed is expulsion from the order. The offence of speaking to a woman, even 'in a secluded place', is of a lower order of seriousness, requiring formal confession of guilt and permitting subsequent restitution of the erring member to the community. The monks, Purchas continues, 'go always barefoot, in poor array, eating nothing but rice and green herbs, which they beg from door to door. They crave it not, nor take it with their hands, but go with a wallet at their backs always, with their eyes modestly fixed on the ground, and calling or knocking, stand still till they receive answer, or something be put in their wallets. Many times they set themselves naked in the heat of the sun . . . They rise at midnight to pray to their Idols, which they do in choirs, as the Friars do. They may not buy, sell, or take any rents, which, if they should do, would bring on them the imputation of heretics' (81:556).

With regard to matters of belief we are told that 'the Siamites
[i.e. the Thais] commonly hold that God created all things,
rewardeth the good and punisheth the bad; that man hath two
spirits; one good, to keep [i.e. to protect); and the other evil,
to tempt, continually attending him'. Cosmological beliefs held by
the Thais appear to have been derived from many nations,
observes Purchas. 'They hold that the world shall last eight
thousand years, whereof six thousand are passed, and then it shall
be consumed with fire; at which time shall be opened in heaven
seven eyes of the sun, which shall dry up the waters and burn up
the earth. In the ashes shall remain two eggs, whence shall come
forth one man and one woman, which shall renew the world.
But there shall be no more salt [water] but fresh rivers and lakes,
which shall cause the earth, without man's labour, to abound in
plenty of good things.' In addition to these more eschatological
beliefs the Thai people believe, says Purchas, in 'seven and
twenty heavens, holding that some of them are (like Muhammad's
Paradise) fraught with fair women, with meats also and drinks,
and that all living things which have souls go thither, even
fleas and lice. And these lousy heavens are allotted to all secular
persons which enter not into their rule and habit of religion' – an
interesting Thai Buddhist variation of the fate suitable for non-
believers. 'They have higher heavens for their priests which live in
wildernesses [the forest-monks, or hermits] ascribing only this
felicity to them, there to sit and refresh themselves with the wind.
And according to the higher merits they assign other higher
heavens among their gods, which have round bellies like bowls, and
so have those that go thither. They hold also that there are
thirteen hells, according to the different demerits of men's sins'
(81:556). Returning to the subject of religious practice, Purchas
tells us that the people 'build many and fair temples and place
in them many images of saints, which sometime lived virtuously
and now are in heaven'. The reference is no doubt to statues
of the Buddha and his disciples such as Ananda, which are
usually found in Buddhist shrines. 'They have one statue fifty
paces long, which is sacred to the Father of men. For they think
that he was sent from above, and that of him were born certain
persons that suffered martyrdom for the love of God. Their priests
are clothed in yellow long garments. (This colour is esteemed holy;
and every yellow thing, for the resemblance which it hath with gold,
and with the sun, is hallowed to God). Besides that which is
before said of their strict orders, they may not nourish hens,

because of their female sex. To drink wine is punished in their priests with stoning. They have many Fasts in the year, but one especially, in which the people frequent the temples and their sermons' – a reference, no doubt, to Vesak or Visakha Puja, the commemoration of the Buddha's birth, enlightenment and full entry into nirvana. 'They have their canonical hours by day and night for their holy things.'

At this point Purchas quotes the testimony of Gaspar da Cruz, a Portuguese Dominican, said to have been the first Christian missionary to have worked in Cambodia; he was there in 1555 but did not stay long, because, so he alleged, he met with opposition from the Buddhist monks. 'He thinks the third part of the land to be priests or religious persons [it should be noted that he includes in this third Brahmans also]. These religious are proud, the inferior worshipping their superiors as gods, with prayer and prostrating. They are reverenced much of the people, none daring to contradict them; so that when our Friar Gaspar preached, if one of those Religious came, and said, "This is good, but ours is better," all his auditors would forsake him' (81:556).

Another Christian missionary whose account of Buddhist belief and practice is quoted by Purchas is Balthasar Sequerius, a Jesuit, who landed at Tenasserim (now southern Burma) in 1606. We are told that he 'passed from thence partly by goodly rivers, partly over cragged and rough hills and forests, stored with rhinoceroses, elephants and tigers (one of which tore in pieces one of their company before his eyes)'. He conferred with the Buddhist monks and learnt that according to generally accepted notions 'there was now no God in the world to govern it; three had been, before, now dead, and a fourth is expected, who deferreth his coming'. With regard to religious practice, the Jesuit recorded that 'they observe their festivals according to the course of the moon; and then open their temples, whither the people resort to do their devotions. These are built strong and stately with art and beauty, having their porches, cloisters, choirs and lower aisles, great chapels being annexed on both sides, and large churchyards. In one of these he saw a statue of eighteen cubits length, dedicated to the great God [that is, presumably, the Buddha]. They are of marvellous abstinence, and think it a great sin to taste wine. In their choirs they have singing men, which after the European fashion sing there, especially in the shutting in of the evening and about midnight. Very early in the morning warning is given for them to go to beg from door to door. They have their funeral [rites] for the dead. The carcasses are burned, being put into painted coffins, with great solemnity (if they be great men) with music and dances and great store of victuals to be bestowed on the Talapoins (monks)' (81: 556f).

The condition of Buddhism in seventeenth-century Burma

The Burmese attacks under King Bayin Naung on the various Thai kingdoms surrounding Burma, and the subsequent reprisals of the Thais in the latter half of the sixteenth century, had serious socially disruptive effects in Burma. The Mons, who more than once took the opportunity to rise in rebellion, were dealt with severely by the Burmese kings, and from about this time began migrating eastwards across the border into Thailand. These migrations became so frequent after a while that the Thai king of Ayudhaya made special provisions along the route for the refugees (30: 180f). In Burma it was a time when 'rumours and evil omens troubled the people, the tutelary *devata* of the towns were said to be departing, and religion was dimmed' (8: 56f), in spite of many efforts that were being made to counter these evils by making offerings to local gods and other popular conventional attempts to make 'merit'.

In some monasteries, however, meditation and scholarship managed to survive these troublesome times. The study of Pali grammar and the Abhidhamma continued. During the seventeenth century a good crop of commentaries on Abhidhamma texts was produced in the monasteries of upper Burma. Translations of these texts into Burmese were also being made. As an example of this work of the Thera (Elder) Agga-dhammalankara may be cited; we are told that this Thera translated into Burmese the meaning of the Kaccayana, the Abhidhammatha-sangha, the Matika, the Dhatukatha, the Yamaka, and the Patthana (88:111). The last three named are the fifth, sixth and seventh books of the Pali Abhidhamma-Pitaka; the Matika is an abstract of the first book of the Abhidhamma-Pitaka (the Dhammasangani), and the Abhidhammatha-sangha is a well-known and much used summary or digest of the Pali Abhidhamma books. The same scholar, at the king's request, composed also a chronicle of kings, the Rajavamsa; he was himself the son of a royal minister (88:112).

Other Pali texts were being translated into Burmese; some of the most eminent scholars were turning their hands to this work during the seventeenth century. Bode suggests the reason for this may possibly have been that there was a wider demand for canonical works in Burmese among the ordinary people; more probably the reason was that the standard of Pali scholarship among the monks had declined, so that many of them could no longer read Pali with ease (8:62). Since Abhidhamma works were being rendered into Burmese, and it is hardly likely that anyone but monks would have had the leisure to master their contents or to make use of this material when they had been translated, the latter seems the more convincing explanation. The decline in Pali scholarship in the Sangha may have been a sign of the disturbed conditions in Burma, especially upper Burma, during the sixteenth and seventeenth centuries.

The ancient home of Buddhism in Burma was the Mon country in the south. This, as we have seen, was suffering from the violence of the Burmese kings, and many Mons were migrating to Thailand. The Burmese had begun to restore their empire from the capital at Toungoo. In 1634 they moved farther north to Ava, in the central Irrawaddy plain. Even when the Mons were not in revolt against the Burmese or were not being punished for it, they had lost touch with the arts of peace and their formerly prosperous land became a stagnant, increasingly deserted area, and the institutional life of Buddhism became looser and increasingly factional. At the end of the seventeenth century a controversy began among the monks which was to continue as a major issue for nearly a century. The subject of the dispute indicates the quality of religious life in the Sangha at that time; the great religious question which exercised the entire Sangha was whether a monk should wear his robe with both shoulders covered or with the right shoulder uncovered. Although the rules in the Pali scriptures in the Vinaya Pitaka make clear that both shoulders should be covered, some Burmese monks, perhaps out of ignorance of the texts or perhaps for some other reason, adopted the practice of leaving the right shoulder uncovered. If it was ignorance it may have been a sign of the decline of Pali scholarship generally; it may have been due, on the other hand, as the Burmese Buddhist chronicle suggests, to excessive pre-occupation with the analytical abstractions of the Abhidhamma Pitaka to the exclusion of the Vinaya Pitaka (88:118). Those who regarded such disarray of dress as sheer negligence and inexcusable were not slow to point this out to their ignorant brethren. The 'one-shoulder' (uncovered) or 'Ekamsika' party, as they became known, did not accept the correction, but claimed that their view of the matter had come to them independently of the written text of the scripture through a certain elder monk named Saddhammacari, who had been to Sri Lanka; it was from there that they had received this tradition, they claimed (88:119). The controversy waged to and fro, with accusation and counter-accusation, and even with attempts by the innovating party to have spurious texts composed to justify their views; or so the Pali scriptural fundamentalists alleged. Eventually the matter became so great a public scandal that a royal decree laid down that every monk was free to please himself; in other words, that both sides were right. But fundamentalists commonly do not accept such ridiculous assertions. For if the sacred text says so and so, how can the denial of so and so also be permitted? This was a vital religious issue, and such vital issues have to be settled properly, especially when, as may have happened in this case, other rivalries (such as that between village monks and forest monks) provide much of the vitality (see 66:59).

The pursuit of this particular issue was rather rudely interrupted, however, by fighting between the Mons and the Burmese, which from 1740 became critical. Nevertheless, the issue was kept alive even throughout this period, ready to be taken up again more actively when the interruption had subsided, as we shall see later.

Alaungpaya, the Burmese Buddha-to-be

The Thai kingdom of Ayudhaya enjoyed a glowing sunset period of twenty-five years before the violent storm of Burmese attack which ended its existence in 1767. The period from 1733 to 1758 under the reign of King Boromakot – or Tammaraja to give him his earlier, official title – was one of peace and tranquillity.

When the Thai king Boromakot died in 1758, Burmese power, which was soon to devastate the city and kingdom of Ayudhaya, was already growing. A new ruler, who called himself Alaungpaya, 'the Great Lord, Buddha-to-be', whose political ambitions were in keeping with the magniloquence of his title, had begun to extend Burmese domination once again over the whole area east of Thailand. He defeated the Shans who had controlled upper Burma, and the Mons in lower Burma. Having defeated the Mons also in May 1755 at the riverside village of Dagon, adjoining the great Shwe Dagon pagoda, he renamed the place 'Yangon' (Rangoon) or 'end of strife', and went in state to do homage to the Buddha at the great pagoda. He was a Theravada king of the classical pattern; expansionist, empire builder, and Sangha supporter. In 1758, the year the king of Ayudhaya died, Alaungpaya was away in the north-west of Burma, conquering the Hindu state of Manipur, in the mountains of eastern India. He had the previous year completed his conquest of the Mon country in lower Burma, devastating much of it in the process. The Burmese owed their civilisation and their religion to the Mons, comments Harvey; 'it was an older and apparently a gentler civilisation', and in the end it succumbed to the warrior Burmese from the north who were convinced that it was *their* destiny to rule the whole territory of what is now called Burma. Alaungpaya's claim to be a future Buddha was popularly accepted, and in return Alaungpaya bestowed largesse upon the monks. Large numbers of monks were invited to the palace to be fed every Buddhist holy day (uposatha), and Pali learning was encouraged on all sides. The question of robe-wearing, on which the Sangha had been so strenuously exercised and bitterly divided, was now brought forward again. Alaungpaya's own monk-teacher Atula belonged to the one-shoulder party. In principle, this meant that his attitude was one of tolerance in the interpretation of the sacred text of the Vinaya, and that he was opposed to the strict and literal fundamentalism of the Parupanu, or 'fully clothed' party. The Sasanavamsa, the nineteenth-century chronicle which tells the story, finds Alaungpaya's support for the one-shoulder party rather an embarrassment, and explains it as being due to his pre-occupation with affairs of state and therefore not having time to go into the matter carefully enough. Alaungpaya issued a decree in favour of the one-shoulder party. The literalists therefore had the choice of either backing down after all they had said about the sacredness of scriptures or resisting the king's decree. The majority found it possible, in the event, to accept the ruling, but a few remained undaunted. One of the resisters was banished, but continued in his defiance. He was summoned back to the king's presence. He obeyed the summons, fully expecting the death sentence. 'So sure was he of the fate awaiting him that he put off his monastic habit before the encounter, with the magnanimous wish to lighten, in some sense, the guilt of the man who would shed his blood' (8:70). It was usual for a Mon to be derobed before being subjected to punishment; for a Buddhist to deal violently with a wearer of the yellow robe would be unthinkable, so in disrobing he was anticipating the king's sentence. In the event he was committed to prison by Alaungpaya. The rest of the story is told rather tersely in the chronicle: 'The king, having put him in prison went to the Siam country for the sake of fighting. But having gone there to fight, he died on his way back' (88:127).

For, in spite of his great vigour, Alaungpaya was a sick man, and his attack on Thailand in 1760 was the last, inglorious event of his life. There was more than one reason for the attack. Partly, it seemed, he could not refrain; he was continually driving himself on to some new conquest. Partly, also, he needed the spoils that would have been his had he succeeded. Having depopulated most of the Mon country of lower Burma, which was now relapsing into jungle, he needed prisoners to settle on his ruined land. Having crossed the hills eastwards he captured a few towns in the western plain of Thailand. As he approached Ayudhaya he showed what he could do by massacring the defenceless local population regardless of age and sex and covering the rivers with their corpses (30:241). Having thus announced himself he added this message in a letter to the king of Ayudhaya: 'His Burmese Majesty comes as a divine incarnation to spread true religion in your country. Come forth with respect and present him with elephants and a daughter' (30:241). The Mon refugees in Ayudhaya told what *they* knew of this divine incarnation, and thereupon the Thais, European *feringhis,* and Muslims together joined in making so resolute a resistance that the ever-conquering king and his army retreated after a few days. The Burmese made for home as fast as they could, but Alaungpaya, now a sick man, died on the way.

The destruction of Ayudhaya in 1767

What Alaungpaya failed to do was achieved by one of his successors seven years later. Ayudhaya was a tempting prize. 'There was gold, silver and jewels in abundance, for the royal treasure was immense. This is the secret of these continual Burmese attacks on Ayudhaya: it was at once a thriving sea-port and a king's palace, one of the wealthiest cities in Indo-China, so that its treasures were a standing temptation to the Burmese hordes' (30:253). So it was that little more than five years after Alaungpaya had died on the retreat from Thailand that a Burmese king, his son and successor, was once again at the head of an army occupying the Menam plain and laying siege to Ayudhaya. After holding out for a year the city fell to the Burmese; it was sacked by them and completely burnt down. The inhabitants fled into the forests or by boat down the river.

A most vivid account of the destruction of Ayudhaya by the Burmese is contained in the report written by a French Catholic missionary, Monseigneur Alary, to his superior in Paris. He describes the approaching sound of the cannon shots in the early hours of the morning, the noise of the advancing army, and his own preparation to leave his house and make for the forest. But Burmese troops were at the door before he could go, 'with spears and torches'. They looted the presbytery and stripped him of all but his shirt and led him outside before setting fire to his house. There is a great deal more concerning the humiliation to which he and his fellow captives were subjected; of their being exposed to the weather and the constant threat of summary death; the weeping and cries of the raped women; and the plundering and burning which continued for some days as the Burmese army behaved after the usual manner of undisciplined and savage troops (Quoted in 43:259–72).

It was not a war of religion. Monseigneur Alary explicitly mentions this fact. It was, however, a case of the Buddhists from one country (Burma) destroying the Buddhists of another (Thailand) for the glory of doing so, for material gain, and for an outlet for their own greed, hatred and delusion *(lobha, dosa,* and *moha)*, the three primary conditions which 'Buddhism' is supposed to undermine. The connection between Buddhist personal ethics and Buddhist nationalist wars will be explored in more detail when our survey of the history reaches the twentieth century.

The Thai kingdom which was destroyed in 1767 was in certain important respects a Buddhist kingdom, but it was not entirely so. The ruined buildings of Ayudhaya include monastic establishments of the type which is still to be seen in Thailand today, especially in Bangkok. The great meeting-hall for monks, the mural paintings illustrating episodes in the life of the Buddha and his disciples and of his earlier existences, the stupa, or chedi, at which devotions are performed, all these certainly were to be found in Ayudhaya, as now in all the large monasteries of Bangkok. In this, the Buddhism of Ayudhaya is seen to be close to the general pattern of classical Sinhalese Buddhism which has become standard throughout South–East Asia. But there are other features which indicate the continuing presence of Khmer culture, such as the style of the statues and the alternative to the stupa, namely the prang, or Khmer-style tower. Politically and culturally, as Coedès has emphasised, Thai Buddhism of the Ayudhaya period is heir to Indian civilisation, but 'Indian' in the form in which the Thais received it from the Khmers rather than from the Sinhalese Theravadins (16:163f).

Buddhist factionalism continued

The reign of one of Alaungpaya's grandsons, Singu (1776–82), reflected the Burmese people's weariness of war. Neither a warrior nor an ambitious Buddhist, he decided to spend his time more enjoyably. He tried a pilgrimage or two but had no great taste for religion and took to the soft life of music, poetry, and drink instead, in the company of young people like himself. Anyone who criticised his way of life he executed (37:185). According to the Burmese chronicle, however, he came strongly under the influence of a very learned monk named Nandamala. This is alleged to have happened as the result of a dream the king had. He saw the god Sakka, wearing a white garment, and adorned with white ornaments and white flowers. He saw Sakka come before the king and heard him say: 'O King, at the foot-shrine on the bank of the Narmada river, in the Aparanta country [that is in Burma], there have grown up many grasses intertwined root with root, stem with stem, and leaf with leaf, and they cover the shrine. These were not cleared away by the former kings, who really had no knowledge of them. But now these should be cleared away by you, as you really know and are anxious, to make them clean.' In the dream a monk came and explained the meaning to the king. On waking, King Singu sent for the elder named Nandamala and asked for an explanation of the dream, and this Nandamala most willingly gave (88:129).

Nandamala was a great authority on matters of monastic discipline. He was therefore a convinced upholder of the traditional manner of wearing robes, a supporter of the fully-clothed party. He took this opportunity to explain to the king the rights and wrongs of the dispute between the traditionalists and the one-shoulder party, and succeeded in convincing the king that the traditionalists were, after all, in the right. In order to demonstrate the matter publicly the king arranged a debate between the two parties. The one-shoulder party was conclusively shown to be acting in contravention of the sacred text, and the king issued a decree ordering all monks to conform to the scriptural regulation henceforth.

This was not the end of the controversy, however. The 'innovators' made further but ill-fated attempts to revive the issue during the reign of the next king, Bodawpaya (1782–1819, not counting an abortive reign of seven days in between). But they were obliged to argue from their opponents' premises, namely the eternal validity of the letter of the sacred law, and on such grounds they could only lose. When the words of an ancient text are exalted to such a position of authority that men's actions are for evermore bound by what was once written, then intellectual flexibility, free inquiry and, indeed, any openness to new possibilities become equated with heresy. Even so, it is important to notice that even the prestigious sacred law is not always sufficient in itself to command agreement and obedience. Sacred law requires sanctions for its enforcement: either in the form of a universal belief in it and acceptance of its eternally binding authority, or sanctions of some other sort. In the case of the Theravada Buddhist law it seems frequently to have needed the sanctions provided by a royal law enforcement officer, for that in effect was one of the important roles of the king in Theravada countries. The Buddhist Sangha in the last resort depended on the king to compel enforcement of its own law. In the last resort it was not the sacred law which counted, but political power.

3
The Clash of Empires:
1782–1900

Burmese Buddhism in the early nineteenth century

The period of King Bodawpaya's reign (1782–1819) has been described as a watershed 'separating Burma's eighteenth century traditionalism from its unavoidable orientation towards the outside world in the nineteenth' (13:68). Bodawpaya was the fourth and in many respects the ablest son of Alaungpaya. He stands in contrast with Singu, whom he succeeded in 1782. Bodawpaya was no lover of peace as Singu had been but a ruler with imperial ambitions, some of which were to have long-lasting consequences for Burmese Buddhism.

The year after his accession he moved the royal capital from what he believed to be the unlucky site at Ava to nearby Amarapura. It was not a move prompted by major strategic, political or economic considerations. If any of these had been regarded as relevant he might have chosen to make Rangoon (which Alaungpaya had established as a provincial capital in the south) the capital of his kingdom. Rangoon is in the delta, on the northern bank of the wide, and fairly deep, Rangoon river, which gives seagoing ships good access to the city. As Harvey points out, 'Rangoon might have let a little fresh air from the outer world into the court. But as the capital was not moved there this did not happen, and so the ideas and outlook of the Burmese kings remained to a large extent that of the upper Burma villages among which their various capitals – Ava, Amarapura, Mandalay – were set', although not quite so entirely as Harvey suggests. 'Their ideas remained in the nineteenth century what they had been in the ninth. To build pagodas, to collect daughters from tributary chiefs, to sally forth on slave raids, to make wars for white elephants – these conceptions had had their day, and a monarchy which failed to get beyond them was doomed.' Harvey points out that in Thailand the trend was in the other direction: the capital was moved successively farther south, finally to the seaport of Bangkok. It is perhaps not a coincidence that Thailand in the nineteenth and twentieth centuries has been less xenophobic and more open to influence from the outside world (30:248f). However, it is possible to see why the Burmese and the Thai rulers chose the sites of their capitals as they did respectively. The Thais in one sense were forced to find a site for a new capital, when Ayudhaya had been destroyed in 1767, and to find one in a situation less exposed to Burmese attack and better able to be defended against it if necessary. Hence the choice of Bangkok on the *east* bank of the wide Menam river. The Burmese were under no immediate obligation of that sort to find a new capital. And, even although Bodawpaya considered it desirable to have his capital differently sited, the idea of moving it to Rangoon would have been strongly resisted. The delta region of lower Burma was the country of the Mons, where the Burmese were conscious of being to some extent aliens. Men who are used to the dry fierce heat of upper Burma will not care for the sultry, humid delta with its excessively high rainfall in the wet season. Bangkok has by comparison a pleasanter climate, and the Thai kings of Ayudhaya, themselves strongly Khmer in their cultural and political tradition, did not have a feeling of being in alien territory in the coastal region, for this was also traditionally the Khmer region.

In the case of the Burmese shift of capital the choice of new site was determined by cultic and astrological considerations. Amarapura was declared to be a more auspicious site than Ava. So the move was made, in accordance with these considerations; that fact is a reminder of the nature of Burmese Buddhism, a nature which, of course, it shared with the Buddhism of neighbouring countries of South–East Asia.

By the beginning of the nineteenth century Bodawpaya had demonstrated the very different character of his rule from that of peace-loving Singu, his predecessor. 'To build pagodas, to collect daughters from tributary chiefs, to sally forth on slave raids, to make wars for white elephants . . .' – these certainly appear to have been his conception of monarchy. In 1784 he had attacked the kingdom of Arakan, bordering East Bengal, and had carried away twenty thousand Arakanese prisoners as slaves, including the king of Arakan. His attack had also sent other Arakanese Buddhists northwards as refugees into Chittagong. Some of them settled down there and added to the Buddhist population of Chittagong. Others, more restless and turbulent, were a cause of disturbance and as such were highly unwelcome to the British, who, from Calcutta, now administered East Bengal, including Chittagong District. It was this fact which brought Burma into contact with British imperial rule for the first time, and thus began forty years of uneasy relations which culminated in the Anglo-Burmese war of 1825.

From Arakan, Bodawpaya carried away also the huge statue of the Buddha from the Maha Muni temple ; he did so, it is said, because he feared the protective power it afforded to the city of Arakan, an emotion perhaps difficult for the modern reader to reconcile with the fact that Bodawpaya had in fact captured the city and the statue. However, in Bodawpaya's view his success was due to his having sent spies in advance, two of whom were qualified in witchcraft and disguised as Buddhist monks. These two had gone to the Maha Muni shrine, worshipped there, and then performed magical rites to ensure the Buddha statue's power would be neutralised (30:267). Once captured, the transporting of this colossal statue, in sections, over the mountain passes into Burma was no mean feat. Today it stands in the Maha Muni Temple in Mandalay, and is known as the Arakan Buddha. Perhaps because of its size, perhaps because of its associations, perhaps because of the dim sombreness of the temple in which it stands (or a combination of all three), it can convey to the modern visitor a deep sense of the numinous quality of Burmese Buddhism. Bodawpaya carried out a series of attacks on Thailand also, and occupied Chiengmai, in the north. The Thais recovered the city in 1802 and forced the Burmese back; the result of this campaign was disastrous and exhausting for the Burmese; much previously cultivated land became jungle, towns became uninhabited, and, inevitably, Buddhist institutions declined in those areas.

Bodawpaya can be said to have had two major preoccupations, military and religious. When he was not engaging in costly wars of territorial expansion he was busy with equally costly pagoda-building programmes, for which, as Cady says, he had a mania (13:69). He believed himself to be a Bodhisattva, or Buddha-to-be (as befitted a great king of Burma), and spent much time in the pursuit of the white elephant cult. To capture a white elephant in the jungle was a matter of great rejoicing; 'he was only technically white, and it needed a trained eye to diagnose him'; nevertheless, once captured there was no sin so grave that could not be more than expunged by the fact of possessing such a mysteriously divine creature, such 'a living sacrament' (30:273f). When it came to sins such as the reckless shedding of blood Bodawpaya was well ahead in a field where competitors were not lacking in South–East Asia. Some of this he did in the name of religion. He persecuted those he considered heretics; he imposed the death penalty for drinking alcohol, for the smoking of opium, or the killing of an ox. The Buddhist Sangha remonstrated, and tried to restrain him and, as a body, the Sangha refused his claim to be a Bodhisattva (7:77). Bodawpaya thereupon announced plans to reorganise the Sangha, and took over many monastic lands as a punishment. The Catholic missionary Father Sangermano, who was in Burma from about 1783 to 1807, begins his account of Bodawpaya with the words: 'I suppose that there is not in the whole world a monarch so despotic as the Burmese emperor' (85:73). However, Bodawpaya was not altogether intolerant, as the presence of the Catholic mission in his kingdom shows. The first Protestant missionaries also arrived from British India during his reign, in 1807. Their names were Marden and Chater, and on reaching Rangoon they found, so the record goes, 'the Government spoken of by everyone they consulted, as exceedingly tolerant in religious matters, and as by no means likely to interfere with attempts to convert its subjects to the Christian faith . . .' (66:20).

Thai Buddhism and the founding of royal Bangkok

The beginning of Bodawpaya's reign in 1782 coincided with the establishing of a new dynasty of Thai kings in a newly selected capital, a village now to become a city known generally as Bangkok. After the destruction of Ayudhaya the defeated Thai king, who had fled into the countryside, eventually starved to death. A Thai general named Phraya Tak, born in Ayudhaya, a son of a Chinese father, escaped with about five hundred men who formed the nucleus of what was to become the new governing class. He established a temporary headquarters at Chanburi, on the eastern coast of the Gulf, and there built up an army of the men who flocked to him from all the towns of the surrounding region. With five thousand troops he sailed inland, northwards up the Menam river to Thonburi (on the western bank, facing modern Bangkok on the eastern bank). For the next fifteen years, until 1782, Thonburi was the temporary capital of the reviving Thai government. The ease with which Buddhist monks moved in and out of secular life is well illustrated in this period. When the government of Ayudhaya ceased to exist, local centres of power emerged throughout the country. In the town of Sawangburi (or Farng) in the northern part of the central plain not far from Sukhodaya, a Buddhist monk named Ruan set himself up as the local ruler, appointing his fellow monks as army commanders and general officers. At Ayudhaya, where he had formerly studied as a monk for many years, he had been recently appointed a Sangharaja, (a term loosely translated as 'bishop', but see also p.33 above). He was therefore well qualified to take over the rule of this local state newly emerging from the ruins of the old (99:99f). A number of other petty states had also arisen, and Phraya Tak saw it as his first task to unite them again into one Thai kingdom.

He saw it also as part of his task of national regeneration to improve the quality of the Sangha. He ordered the monks to undergo severe physical tests to prove their purity and moral strength. However, he himself by about 1777 began to show signs of eccentricity; some have called it insanity; he claimed to have become an arahant (or saint), and demanded appropriate tokens of respect from the senior monks. His general Phraya Chakri eventually took over control and in 1782 moved the capital across the Menam to Bangkok. Chakri was acclaimed king, took the title of King Rama, and became, what could not be foreseen in those uncertain days, the founder of a great dynasty that has continued for nearly two centuries, until the present time.

He, too, turned his attention very soon to the affairs of the Sangha, so central a place did the Buddhist order hold in the national life. One of his first undertakings was to commission a complete new edition of the Pali Tipitaka, the cost of which was borne by the royal purse. A revised edition had to be made six years later, however, in 1788, as it was found that there were numerous errors in the edition of 1782. The council which produced the revised edition is reckoned in Thailand to be the ninth 'Buddhist Council', the first having taken place in India shortly after the parinibbana of the Buddha; the second and third also occurred in India; the fourth, fifth, sixth and seventh are held to have taken place in Sri Lanka; and the eighth in Chiengmai in the year 1477 CE, when it was a great centre of Pali scholarship. It has to be noted that the last four of these are not universally accepted even in the Theravada countries as full Councils, for the chanting of the entire Tipitaka is required in a Council, and this was not the case in the later Sinhalese and the Thai so-called 'Councils'. The council held in Thailand in 1788 is .sometimes called the second Buddhist Council of Thailand. It took place at Wat Mahathat in Bangkok and lasted for five months. The Supreme Patriarch of Thailand presided over a gathering of two hundred and eighteen monks and thirty-two lay scholars (57:78).

Another matter with which Rama I concerned himself was the standardisation of a. code of morality for monks. He issued numerous decrees in order to establish proper standards of conduct, not only for monks but for lay people as well. He regarded this as particularly necessary in order to remedy the decline in standards which the recent period of political turmoil had entailed. Under the tenth decree, issued in 1801, over a hundred monks were arrested, laicised, and sent to hard labour as punishment for continual disregard of the required standards of morality. The charge against them was as follows:

> Certain monks, taking advantage of their honourable standing, are so shameless as to descend to all kinds of low behaviour such as drinking intoxicants . . . wandering out at night to see entertainments, rubbing shoulders with women . . . engaging in loose talk . . . boarding Chinese junks in order to obtain fancy objects of merchandise, thus rendering themselves objects of scorn and ridicule to foreign unbelievers. Some go to Phrabad, where they while away their days in flirting with women excursionists and adopt at night the highwayman's life or attend low and undignified entertainments . . . (20:24).

The king built or restored a total of twelve wats, or monasteries, in Bangkok in addition to the wat in the grounds of the royal palace, namely, Wat Po. He showed a very great interest in the revival of Thai literature, and himself contributed notably to it. One of his most renowned contributions was a complete translation into Thai of the Indian religious epic, the Ramayana, a story which has become deeply embedded in the popular culture of Thailand. An incomplete translation had been made in the preceding reign. The king encouraged the translation into Thai of Chinese literary works also, one of the most famous being the *Romance of the Three Kingdoms* (44:196–203). The magnificence of the monastery buildings in Bangkok and the extent of the classical literature which date from this period indicate how vigorous was royal Buddhism during the closing years of the eighteenth century, on the eve of what was perhaps to be its most splendid period in Thai history.

Thai Buddhism in the early nineteenth century

Having refused to retaliate when the Burmese armies of Bodawpaya invaded Thailand, and to attempt any invasion of Burma by way of reply, King Rama I of Bangkok succeeded in what he set out to do, namely to consolidate his kingdom. His policy had long-term consequences of a beneficial kind for Thailand, just as Bodawpaya's policy had long-term consequences of the opposite sort for Burma and the Burmese Sangha. By 1800 Thailand was well on the way to recovery from the Burmese invasions and was stronger than ever before.

The second reign in the Bangkok dynasty, that of Rama II, began in 1809, and was a time of further consolidation generally and of the Buddhist Sangha. More monasteries were built, or extended, as in the case of Wat Arun, the famous Temple of the Dawn on the west bank of the Menam, at Thonburi. A wat was already in existence here when King Phraya Tak set up his headquarters at Thonburi in 1767, and had in fact been incorporated into the precincts of the royal palace. It then became a chapel royal and ceased to be a place of residence for monks. When the capital was transferred to Bangkok it became once again a normal wat with accommodation for monks. During Rama II's reign an ambitious work of reconstruction was undertaken; so ambitious, in fact, that it was not completed until the next reign.

An interesting memorial in this wat commemorates an event of an unusual kind which occurred here in 1817. A Thai by the name of Nai Nok who used often to meditate at Wat Arun told his relatives that he had decided to perform an act of self-immolation in honour of the Buddha. This practice, which became well known during the 1960s in connection with the war in Vietnam, seems to have had its origin in the devotional act of burning a light in honour of the Buddha, an act which was regarded as meritorious. There is a story in the Mahayana scriptures (the Saddharma-pundarika Sutra) of a Bodhisattva who ate incense and drank oil for twelve years and then after bathing in oil set fire to himself as an offering to the Buddha. There are various examples of the occurrence of the practice among Chinese Buddhists between the fifth and tenth centuries; it was this which was thus revived in modern times by the Thai Buddhist, Nai Nok. His was not the first case, however, in modern South–East Asia. A similar case, which occurred in 1790, is commemorated in the same wat, and it seems possible that the record of this on a commemorative tablet in the wall of the sanctuary may have influenced Nai Nok. The earlier immolation was performed by a Thai named Nai Ruang, who meditated for a while at Wat Arun and then covered himself with oil and set fire to himself. The two events are commemorated by seated stone figures, one on the north and one on the south side of the sanctuary (10:58f).

During the reign of Rama III (1824–51) a reform movement began in Thai Buddhism. This took the form of a yet stronger emphasis on the orthodox attitudes and practices set out in the Pali sacred texts and has to be seen against the background of popular religion in Thailand as it existed then and as it exists now. It was a movement which can in general be characterised as a strengthening of royal or political Buddhism at the expense of popular Buddhism, an enhancement of what was rational in Thai Buddhist culture, arising from an induced sense of embarrassment at what was irrational in it.

Christian challenge and Buddhist reform in Bangkok (1824–1851)

One of the commonest results of Christian missionary enterprise in Asia was something the missionaries did not intend or expect: a 'reform' in the religion they were challenging. In India, Ceylon and Burma, Christian missionaries established themselves on a regular basis from the opening years of the nineteenth century, and in each case a reform movement in the existing religion of the country concerned occurred during, broadly speaking, the middle decades of the century. It was so in Thailand also.

Although there had been a Catholic mission in Thailand from the seventeenth century it did not operate continuously and for long periods fell into abeyance. It was not until 1830 that Christian missionary activity of a regular and sustained kind began in Thailand, when the Catholic mission was re-formed on a permanent basis. Protestant missionaries, the first of whom reached Thailand in 1828, began their activities in earnest in 1833. The

Protestants soon took up active progagandist work, preaching and giving out tracts and portions of the Bible in Thai. They used other media also, primarily medical missions and schools (115:35f). At first they concentrated their efforts on the Chinese population of Bangkok, but later extended the medical and educational missions to the Thais also. In connection with their medical work they introduced vaccination against smallpox and in connection with the second they established the first printing-press in Bangkok in 1835.

During this period the king's younger half-brother, Mongkut, was studying as a Buddhist monk. At the death of Rama II it was he as the legitimate heir who would normally have become king. But in 1824 Mongkut was only twenty years old and had just entered the Buddhist order. It was decided that he should remain a monk; and that his half-brother, who was not technically eligible for the succession (as his mother was not, like Mongkut's, a royal lady), should nevertheless become king. Mongkut therefore continued in the Sangha for another twenty-seven years until at Rama III's death he himself eventually became king of Thailand.

In the intervening years it was he who was largely responsible for inaugurating a reform in Thai Buddhist life in Bangkok. Vella regards this as having been due largely to 'the challenge of Christianity', and Mongkut as the man ideally suited and in the best position to lead a Buddhist reform movement (115:38). He had a keen, critical mind. At the beginning of his life in the Sangha he lived at a wat which at that time was outside the city where 'forest monks' specialised in meditation. But he became discouraged by what he quickly discovered to be the pedantic attitude of teachers of meditation; they became supercilious or angry at questions from students (87:49). He left there to return to the city monastery, Wat Mahathat, and took to the study of the Pali scriptures, in which he became highly proficient. The result of his researches into the canonical Pali texts, however, was to make clear to him the discrepancy between the Buddhism of the ancient texts and the Buddhism of nineteenth-century Thailand. Manifestly they were not the same (as often happens in the progress of living religions), but ideally they should be, he thought (as protestant reformers often do). For a while he felt very depressed about the situation, and was on the point of renouncing his ordination as member of a Sangha which he now felt to be a sham. Then he met a Mon Buddhist monk from Thonburi, who restored his faith in the Sangha by demonstrating to him the manner of life of the Mon Buddhists, which appeared to Mongkut to be much closer to the ideal set out in the scriptures (20: 31). He thereupon obtained re-ordination from the Mon monks, went back to his original wat on the outskirts of Bangkok, and there began to gather a school of monks like himself who sought to live strictly in accordance with the Buddha's Dhamma. They became known as the Dhammayut monks – those who adhere to the Dhamma, or law (of the Buddha). The new sect was opposed to what they understood as the 'non-Buddhist' accretions which had come to be part of Thai Buddhism, namely the cults of the *phi* and the *chao*, the spirits of the dead; the cults of Brahmanical gods, the Nagas and demons, the gods Indra, Vishnu, Shiva and Rama; the practices of spirit-doctors, prophets, magicians, astrologers, cabbalists and so on.

Mongkut was doubly sensitive to the contrast between this kind of folk religion and the rationalism of the Pali texts because of his association with leading Christian missionaries in Bangkok. Indeed, this probably made him more conscious of what he thought to be the 'rational' and 'anti-magical' nature of the Pali texts than is justified by the texts themselves. He was on good terms with two of the American missionaries, Bradley and Caswell, with whom he studied English, and with the Catholic bishop Pallegoix, who taught him Latin, in return for which Mongkut taught the bishop Pali. His connection with the Mon monks was looked on askance by some of the Thai aristocrats, some of whom openly expressed their disapproval of such associations on the part of a member of the royal family. This provides interesting evidence of the low social status which was ascribed to the Mons by the upper class in Bangkok. However, his half-brother the king encouraged and supported him in his religious and educational activities, and in 1837 made him the abbot of Wat Bovoranives in Bangkok.

This royal wat in the heart of the city thenceforward became the centre of the reformed sect of the Sangha, the Dhammayutika.

The purpose of the Dhammayutika sect was, primarily, to purge the Thai Sangha of what were thought to be un-Buddhist practices, that is to say the sort of practices associated with magic, astrology and the occult which have just been mentioned, and the common practices of folk religion in many parts of the world. It was also, secondarily, to promote what were held to be the more 'correct' practices of the Mon monks with regard to such matters as the manner of wearing robes, carrying the alms-bowl, the rite of ordination, the method of pronouncing Pali, the choice of dates for holy days, and the robe-giving ceremony. Another feature of the reform of practice was the adoption of a new manner of celebrating Vesak, the annual festival commemorating the Buddha's birth, enlightenment and parinibbana. Finally a great reformation of monastic literature was undertaken; commentaries were scrutinised to see whether they expressed sound canonical views; if they did not, and if they incorporated popular 'myths', they were rejected as unsuitable for monastic use (115:40). The preference was always for whatever was rational, the intention was 'to bring the Buddhist religion into accordance with the scientific thought that was emanating from the West'. There was also a change of emphasis regarding the purpose of the Sangha's life: 'Under the influence of Christianity, the new sect also attempted to change the outlook of Buddhism from concentration on the monastic life to concentration on enlightening the people' (115:41). Under the same influence sermons were expected to be simpler and more direct, such as the ordinary people could understand.

However, while the Dhammayutika sect was influential in high places because it was primarily a Bangkok sect, this fact had also a somewhat limiting effect. It remained, for some time at least, primarily a Bangkok movement, and only slowly extended its influence outside the capital. It was, and still is, unrepresentative of the Thai Sangha as a whole, the vast majority of whom live outside the capital and adhere to the traditional Thai Buddhist forms and practices of the Mahanikaya.

Mongkut eventually left Wat Bovoranives to become King of Thailand in 1851. A year later Mindon Min succeeded to the Burmese throne at Amarapura. The two kings reigned as contemporaries for the next sixteen years, that is until Mongkut's death. They were not unlike; each was peaceable, progressive and concerned for the welfare of his respective kingdom; each sought to follow the path of Buddhist Dhamma and to accrue merit. Yet, while for Thailand in the 1850s and 1860s the future was to be one of increasing stability and national integration, for Burma the reverse was true, and the sombre shadow of Burma's coming time of troubles could already be perceived by the end of Mindon's reign. In Thailand, state Buddhism was to continue to flourish; in Burma it was to suffer the kind of assault against which neither the Burmese people, nor their king, nor the Sangha could defend it.

Mindon: a pious Buddhist king of Burma (1852–1878)

A quarter of a century or so earlier, in 1825, two expanding empires had met in the Arakan region in north-west Burma: the Burmese under their aggressive king Bagyidaw (pronounced Ba-jee-daw) and the British, who by this time were strongly established in Bengal. The result had been Burma's loss of the Arakan and, by way of indemnity, the coastal area of Tenasserim in the south also. The loss of this territory in the first Anglo-Burmese War had been followed in 1852 by further losses, notably the whole of lower Burma, including the ports of Rangoon and Pegu, in the second Anglo-Burmese War. It was in this situation of crisis that Mindon Min became king in the capital in upper Burma, Amarapura. The Mons in lower Burma, with the Karens, who were kindred spirits in their dislike of Burmese overlordship, had seized the opportunity provided by the Burmese king's pre-occupation to rise in revolt. They were savagely punished for it by the Burmese subsequently, on the grounds that they had aided the British. But the grandiose plans of Bodawpaya and Bagyidaw to extend Buddhist Burma northwards and westwards were in ruins by the end of the first quarter of the nineteenth century and Mindon Min inherited a circumscribed kingdom and a delicate political situation.

The various measures which he took, as a Buddhist king, may be seen in more than one light. For although he succeeded to a diminished kingdom he entertained the hope that the British occupation of Arakan and lower Burma might be only temporary (124: 76–8). His diplomatic relations with the British were, therefore, conducted with discreet dignity and caution. Even when the sun of British imperial good fortune was overclouded by troubles in the Crimea in 1854–6 (with consequent predictions that Russia would win, and would force Britain out of India, and out of Burma) and by troubles nearer at hand in the Sepoy Rebellion of 1857, Mindon carefully refrained from doing anything to embarrass or antagonise the British. In the perspective of the righteous Buddhist ruler his policies can be seen as having been intended to gain merit. He sought to do so in other ways also. For example, he set about improving the general condition of the Sangha, a worthy aim in itself for a Buddhist monarch, and one which also had the temporal advantage of improving the general condition of his kingdom. The attempts he made to purify the Sangha and tighten its discipline, and to encourage pious and learned monks to return to British-occupied lower Burma were consistent with his expectation that the territory would one day revert to him and with the desire that when this happened what he would reinherit should be a worthy part of a Buddhist kingdom. He was very active in adding fresh adornment to the Shwe Dagon pagoda in Rangoon, and this too can be seen in the same light. Partly it would accrue to him as merit, partly it would serve to remind the Mon and Karen peoples of the delta region that they were, rightfully, subjects of the Buddhist king in Amarapura.

There was in fact something of a mild revival of Buddhism in Burma in Mindon's reign. It was not altogether a spontaneous revival; it did not arise from within the nature of the Buddhist kingdom; rather it appears to have had a lot to do with the fact that there was an aggressive imperialist power in the offing, a monster to be appeased and placated, and even, if possible, persuaded to go away. It is not necessary to decide between the two explanations of Mindon's conduct of affairs, that is whether it was piety or self-preservation that prompted him, as if they were alternatives. If he had been a less wise man he could very easily have brought disaster upon his kingdom in the form of British conquest and annexation some thirty years sooner than it actually happened (under his son, Thibaw). Undoubtedly he was, as Cady says, 'devoutly religious, a man of high character, well-mannered and well intentioned, opposed to bloodshed, incapable of trickery', a king who 'won the respect of the neighbouring British authorities as a man of integrity and progressive capabilities' (13:99f). During his reign, therefore, Buddhism in Burma had an opportunity of recovery and of re-rooting itself where it had been before displaced. The Burmese chronicle, the *Sasanavamsa*, records during his reign a new enthusiasm among not only the monks but the lay people also; religious studies were carried out with new vigour, and Buddhist precepts observed with new zeal. So much new literary work in Pali was done in Burma in Mindon's reign that Bode sees the nineteenth century in this respect linked with the twelfth, and the history of Pali literature repeating itself (7:93). Once again royal Buddhism showed itself as the patron and promoter of Pali orthodoxy.

Another of Mindon's religious works was the convening of a great council in the newly built city of Mandalay (founded in 1857) to rehearse, as in olden times, the entire text of the Tipitaka, and so to restore the best readings and establish the accepted text. After this had been done, in 1872, the entire text was engraved on marble slabs which were then set up in the capital. In this way Mindon gained for himself the title of 'Convenor of the Fifth Council' (so the number is reckoned in Burma), a title which he is said to have valued above any other. Maung Htin Aung comments that he was 'one of the ablest kings that Burma ever had' (37:233).

Buddhist ecclesiasticism in nineteenth-century Burma

An account of Buddhist life in Burma during the reign of King Mindon is contained in the Pali chronicle entitled *Sasanavamsa*, already referred to in passing. This is the work of the king's own tutor, the monk Pannasami, whose account of Burmese Buddhist history takes the reader as far as the year 1860, three years after the founding of the city of Mandalay by King Mindon. As the author says, in almost the last words of his account: 'This is the founding of the *Sasana* in the city of Ratana punna [i.e. Mandalay]' (88: 164).

The '*Sasana*', whose history he had been writing, the *Sasana* which he had now seen established in the new capital city of Mandalay, consisted of a particular pattern of relationships between Burmese king and Buddhist monks in which Pannasami himself had a special interest. Elsewhere in his chronicle he declares that 'under the patronage of the righteous kings this religion of the supreme Buddha [*Sammasambhuddhassa sasanam*] in the Maramma country [Burma] was made to shine greatly, and it came to growth, prosperity and full development. And the religion as it is called [*sasanan ca nam etam*] endures under the patronage of kings'. He adds that its prosperity was not only the work of kings, but of all the loyal people as well: 'also all the inhabitants of the kingdom, who were obedient to their kings, and supported by the righteous kings, were the helpers of the religion [*sasanass' upakara*]'.

The word *sasana* is here given a somewhat more specialised meaning than that which it bears in the canonical literature, where it means, generally, 'the message', or 'teaching' or 'instruction', or 'doctrine of the Buddha'.* From that primary meaning a more specialised usage follows, in which the 'ninefold Buddha – sasana' is spoken of; this is a way of distinguishing nine types of canonical literature in which the doctrine is contained (76: 150).

---

*For example Digha Nikaya I, 110; II, 206; Sutta Nipata 482, etc.

The word *sasana* as it is used by Pannasami, however, clearly indicates a particular kind of Buddhist polity. Sometimes *sasana* is virtually equivalent to 'Sangha', as in the account of the reform of the Sangha by Mindon in 1858, when the king asks who, in the *Buddha – sasana*, are the monks and novices whose way of life does not conform with the Vinaya (88:154). At other times it appears to indicate as we have first seen a polity which kings and lay people also co-operate in building up.

It is in the *sasana* in this sense that Pannasami's interest appears to lie. It is this which he sets out to chronicle: 'the history of the *sasana* in the Aparanta country', that is in Burma. In doing so, one of his major concerns is to show that orthodoxy has to be distinguished from unorthodoxy, and it is quite clear that he regards himself as tutor of the king and chief Buddhist monk, as representing orthodoxy. Since the king's teacher was holder of the title 'head of the sasana', or in Burmese *thathana-baing,* it is evident that the royally supported Buddhist establishment was regarded as representing orthodoxy. This term was well known to the French bishop, Bigandet, who recorded in a work written and published in Burma in Mindon's reign, in 1866, that the keystone of the Buddhist fabric

is the superlatively great master residing in the capital or its suburbs. His jurisdiction extends over all the fraternity within the realm of his Burmese Majesty. His position near the seat of Government and his capacity of king's master, or teacher, must have at all times conferred upon him a very great degree of influence over all his subordinates. He is honoured with eminent title of *Thathanapain,* meaning that he has power and control over all that appertains to Religion. It does not appear that peculiarly shining qualifications or high attainments are required in him who is honoured with such dignity. The mere accidental circumstance of having been the king's instructor when he was as yet a youth, is a sufficient, nay, the only necessary recommendation for the promotion to such a high position. Hence it generally happens that each king, at his accession to the throne, confers the highest dignity of the order to his favourite phongyie (6:501).

It was this fortuitous way of making *thathanabaings* that the British administrators in Burma after the annexation of 1885 were not in a position to appreciate. As we shall see later, part of the trouble over the appointment of a new *thathanabaing* was that the British governor was too conscientious in trying to get, as he thought, the right man.

The system within which the *thathanabaing* functioned was one which can be described as royal state Buddhism, or in the sense in which the word is used by Pannasami, the *sasana*. It was a system in which the king had become the final authority in ecclesiastical affairs, as Mabel Bode observed on the evidence of the *Sasanavamsa* (8:54), and in which the higher members of the Sangha had 'become councillors of State or dignitaries of a Church supported and enriched by royal bounty'. But also, at the lower levels especially, the monks acted as a 'social force, an upholder of humanity and justice against barbaric tyranny, a grave, strenuous influence in the midst of a careless people' (8:58). This function the monks continued to fulfil after the British usurpation of royal power, and in spite of the absence of an effective *thathanabaing*. So far as the royal system and its exalted Buddhist officials were concerned, however, Bode comments that there was 'in the religious History of *Mramma* a striking departure from the Master's [that is, the Buddha's] conception of the true *Samana*, the monk-philosopher, with his intense spirituality . . . and his detachment from all' (8:57).

It was a system in which the Buddhist monk depended to a very large degree for his well-being upon the king's power. Such was the nature of this royal power that it amounted to despotism, sometimes benevolent, sometimes not, and under such rule 'no man's property or labour is his own; the means of supporting the Sangha may be withdrawn from any subject who is under the royal displeasure'. Thus, Bode points out, 'the peaceful, easy life dear to the Burmese bhikkhu, the necessary calm for study or the writing of books, the land or water to be set apart for ecclesiastical ceremonies (a fitting place for which is of the highest importance), all these are only secured by the king's favour and protection'. In her view it is this which explains 'the general loyalty of the Sangha to the head of the State'. But it is not certain that all monks were subject to ecclesiastical authority or supported this royal Buddhism. Pannasami himself gives plenty of evidence of 'dissident' monks who refused to bow to official rulings made by *thathanabaing* and king in concert, as, for one example, in the famous robe-wearing controversy (8:53).

Pannasami's interest was, as we have noted, to emphasise the distinction between orthodoxy and unorthodoxy among Buddhist monks. This is in itself also an acknowledgement that monks in Burma in the middle of the nineteenth century differed considerably in their views of what it was to be a Buddhist. In this version of the matter orthodoxy consisted in the ability to prove one's position by showing that it was derived from some great Buddhist teacher of the past, by the only recognised method for doing so, which was appeal to the canonical Pali texts. As in many other cases in the history of religion the politicisation of religion is accompanied by the need for a definitive standard of orthodoxy, in order to try to ensure unity within the ranks of the professionals of the state religion. Such orthodoxy is likely to be in greater or lesser degree arbitrary, and possibly even a matter of historical chance. It becomes in effect a type of prejudice, and can sometimes be very rigid. Certainly, as Bode recognises, there are woven into Pannasami's work considerable 'orthodox prejudices' (8:57). His historical record is one-sided and is marked by some glaring and significant omissions. What is perhaps most indicative of the fact that here we get a picture of only one element in the Buddhist religious life of Burma in the nineteenth century, alongside which it is necessary to set others, is the writer's apparent total lack of interest in what may be called popular religion, even of a Buddhist kind. We 'rarely hear of popular movements and feelings', Bode comments in her Introduction (8:57).

Yet it is certain that there were other varieties of Buddhist religion. By his concern for orthodoxy against unorthodoxy Pannasami tacitly recognises this; other witnesses are more positive and explicit. As a modern Burmese writer puts it, 'Buddhism had never in any place been a single canonical religion and Burmese Buddhism was no exception'. Every monk was encouraged 'to debate any point of doctrine or monastic usage, and only when the discussions resulted in serious controversy did it become necessary for the whole congregation of monks to vote and to express the view of the majority. Even at that point, the minority could leave the congregation and form a group of their own' (36:14f).

The existence of such variety as would be likely to result from the working of this principle is well attested. Michael Mendelson in particular has emphasised this, especially in his recent work, *Sangha and State in Burma*. Moreover, Mendelson's own fieldwork in Burma in 1958–9 was effective in revealing the existence of Buddhist 'Messianic' associations, or *gaings*, which, since their basis is one which runs back into the medieval period, are likely to have been a feature of Burmese Buddhist life for some centuries, even although they did not receive much mention in written documents, at least until the British period. There was, moreover, what he has called the 'passive' Sangha, that is, communities of monks who were content to take the Vinaya as their sole arbiter, and to dispense with any royal patron or controller (62, 63, 64, 65).

On the basis of all these considerations, Mendelson would seem to be justified in concluding that 'the *thathanabaing* was never regarded by the whole, fundamentally ungovernable, Sangha as its head' (66: 195). And it is clear that while one kind of religion, the royal state Buddhism or *sasana,* in which Pannasami had a vested interest, had 'endured under the patronage of kings' this by no means constituted the Buddhist community in Burma in its entirety. What has befallen Buddhist religion in Burma in the modern period cannot, therefore, be regarded simply as a question of what befell the *sasana* in 1885 and afterwards. It is this latter question which has monopolised much of the discussion of the condition of Buddhist religion in Burma during the period of British rule and after. A better balance needs to be struck between this one element and others which are equally important, notably those which existed outside the network of royal Buddhism; local Buddhist communities, independent, not conforming to state orthodoxy, but possibly more faithful to the Vinaya in some cases, or to the essential conceptions of the Buddha-sasana in India.

Two monk reformers of Mindon's reign call for special mention. One of these was the Ngettwin Sayadaw (the latter word is, in Burma, a very respectful title for a teacher), who was tutor to Mindon's chief queen. The popular practice of using flowers, candles and incense in personal devotions at a Buddhist shrine was criticised by this Sayadaw. Especially in a great shrine such as the Shwe Dagon pagoda in Rangoon this was to be discouraged, he said, for the faded and dying flowers left by earlier worshippers, and the burnt-out candles and incense sticks, dirtied and spoilt a place which was meant primarily for meditation, and this was what really mattered. What was more, he alleged, in a practical vein, this kind of litter attracted rats, who then made holes and undermined the foundations of the pagoda (perhaps one needs to have lived in Rangoon and seen the size of its rats to understand how serious a threat this might be). The Ngettwin Sayadaw took an unconventional attitude also towards the kind of observance of Buddhist holy days which is usual in Theravada countries, where the upasaka, or 'lay follower' (that is one of more than ordinary devotion), keeps special precepts instead of the normal five for lay people; one of the extra three is to fast from midday on the sabbath for the rest of the day. This he said was unnecessary, and so too was the law of celibacy for a lay devotee. He insisted that what really mattered was the serious and disciplined practice of meditation; earnest lay people should give their serious attention to this.

Another reformer in Burma at this period was the Okpo Sayadaw. This learned monk from Okpo, in the Mon country of lower Burma then occupied by the British, began to teach the largely forgotten idea that the Buddhist Sangha did not need the patronage or the protection of the secular arm. It needed only the Vinaya, and the serious intention among the members of the Sangha to obey the Vinaya as their teacher and master.(a point which, in fact, the texts themselves make quite clear). He urged also that in the keeping of Buddhist precepts the mental attitude was even more important than the deed itself, and that keeping the letter of the law without having the spirit of the law was of little effect; it was the mental attitude which determined whether a deed was meritorious or not. His teaching caused a considerable controversy throughout the country; for to declare that the Sangha did not, after all, need its traditional law enforcement officer, the king, in addition to the law itself was not a view which would commend itself to the king, nor to those monks who sought the king's favour and had retreated to upper Burma when the delta region fell into the hands of the British. Okpo Sayadaw was one of the minority who stayed behind in lower Burma, concerned to maintain the Sasana among the people there. The idea that it was the mental attitude behind an act which mattered most was not disputed by the Okpo Sayadaw's critics; what they wished to maintain was that for simple people, in the early stages of Buddhist devotion, it was wrong to expect too much; it was enough at that stage that the established ritual actions and words were used (36:22f).

There is a certain similarity between the kind of reform of Buddhist practice and teaching which Mongkut initiated in Thailand and the reform in Burma in the reign of Mindon which has just been described. It is tempting to suppose that the rather 'protestant' nature of the Ngettwin and the Okpo Sayadaw's reforms in Burma owed something, as Mongkut's Dhammayutika reforms in Thailand almost certainly did, to the presence of American Protestant Christian missionaries in both these countries in the nineteenth century. The writer's own experience, when living in Burma, of the almost total absence of communication or knowledge of each other between the two communities, the Buddhist Sangha and the Christian missionaries, discourages any conclusion of this sort if it is not supported by very positive evidence. In Burma it is possible that it was the nature of the situation in which the Buddhist Sangha found itself in the 1850s that led to the formulation of these new emphases in Buddhist thought and teaching and practice in lower Burma. Here and there members of the Sangha were being stirred to respond to the new conditions created by the British occupation of the land with new initiatives of their own.

The end of the Burmese Buddhist kingdom (1878–1885)

The fortunes of the Buddhist state in Burma and in Thailand respectively began to diverge very sharply in the period we are now to consider, namely the last two decades of the nineteenth century and the first decade or so of the twentieth. In Thailand these years were part of the long reign of King Chulalongkorn (1868–1910), and were a period of steady strengthening of the central power of the Thai state, whereas in Burma this was a period in which the Burmese Buddhist kingdom came into final conflict with British colonial expansion and in 1885 was destroyed. Whether, or to what extent and in what ways, Buddhist tradition in Burma was adversely affected in consequence is an important question we shall have to consider.

There was, as we have noted, a revival of some of the public aspects of Buddhist religion during the reign of King Mindon during the middle decades of the nineteenth century, both in the territory which remained within the Burmese kingdom and in British-occupied lower Burma. When Mindon died in September 1878 palace intrigue in Mandalay had ensured that in his place an inexperienced youth named Thibaw was placed on the throne. Thibaw was the son of one of Mindon's wives, a Shan princess, but there were doubts as to who was his father. When Thibaw's birth to the Shan princess was announced King Mindon made inquiries of the official whose duty it was to keep a record of the king's visits to his queens, whereupon it was found that a royal visit had not been made to this particular lady for some years (94:31f). As the son of a disgraced and divorced mother, therefore, Thibaw since his boyhood lived a life of relative obscurity as a

Buddhist monk, and was virtually unknown. It was this fact which commended him to another of the queens, Sinpyumashin, as a candidate for marriage to her daughter, Supayalat. This ambitious and scheming mother had borne the king daughters but no son. As Thibaw was a political nonentity, with no faction supporting him (which other princes with better claims to the throne might have had), he was from the time of his marriage to Supayalat entirely under the control of his mother-in-law; so too was his mother the Shan princess, who had been befriended by the ambitious queen. These two persuaded Thibaw at his accession that in order to ensure that no other contenders for the throne were able to challenge or depose him he should have all possible rivals murdered. John Nisbet, a British government officer in Burma throughout this period, records that despite the more humane counsels of the Burmese chief minister in Mandalay and other officials, and contrary to what might have been expected in view of Thibaw's mild nature and early religious training, the new king gave orders for the massacre to take place on the night of 15 February 1879. The executioners were ruffians who had been released from jail in order to make room for the royal prisoners who were to be slaughtered.

Excited with drink they killed their victims with bludgeons, and strangled with their hands those who still had the strength left to utter cries. The bodies of the women and children were thrown into the pit prepared in the jail, while on the following night eight cartloads of the corpses of the Princes were removed from the city by the western gate, and thrown into the Irrawaddy, according to custom (74:43).

The massacre was continued on the following two nights. Mr Shaw, the British Resident, protested to the Burmese royal ministers against the killings, and managed to save two of the chief princes who had taken refuge in the Residency, and subsequently to transport them via Rangoon to safety in Calcutta. Even there Burmese agents pursued the two princes in an attempt to assassinate them, but finding that they were being watched by the police there they gave up and went back to Mandalay. The 'customary' nature of this sort of massacre among the Burmese on the occasion of a new king's accession was the reason given by the Burmese in answer to the British Resident's protest: 'such "clearing-away" matters must remain at the discretion of any independent Government', so it was said (91:36). The modern Burmese historian, Maung Htin Aung, records the excuse given by the admirers of the Burmese minister, Kinwun Mingyi, namely that he was 'a liberal statesman and a learned judge' who 'wanted a weak king on the throne so that he could take necessary measures to transform the kingdom into a constitutional monarchy' (37:253). G. E. Harvey also mentions this element in the story, and comments that, ironically, it was due to Mindon that Kinwun Mingyi and one or two others had conceived the idea of a constitutional monarchy and of a weak king as the means of establishing it. For Mindon, as a wise and progressive-minded king, 'had sent his ministers to Europe, the first Burmans ever to see the outer world. They were thrilled, and they returned with their minds set on reform, on restricting the royal prerogative.' It was for this reason, according to Harvey, that when 'a feline clique in the harem determined to put their own particular pet on the throne' the progressive ministers agreed to the proposal, for the alternative candidates were mature men with strong views, whereas what these reformist ministers wanted was 'something malleable' (32:21). In this view of the events of February 1879, however, the 'massacre of the Kinsmen' (a Burmese tradition which had for some reigns been in abeyance) was a consequence which had not been foreseen by the ministers and was carried out without their approval; when it was done, Thibaw, fearing that they would therefore attempt to replace him, ordered the ministers themselves to be replaced by others of his own choosing, according to Harvey.

The reader may object that Thibaw's conduct was incompatible with the expressed intention of a Buddhist to refrain from taking life. The objection is well founded. Thibaw provides an excellent illustration of the moral dilemma of a Buddhist who was also an absolute monarch. The manner in which he found it necessary to secure his position as a monarch illustrates the incompatibility which exists between the canonical Buddhism of the scriptures and the inevitable violence which the exercise of monarchical power entails. Perhaps it was for this kind of reason, among others, that the Buddha is represented in the early tradition as regarding kingship as incompatible with the pursuit of Dhamma.

Under Thibaw and his new ministers. the condition of the Burmese kingdom deteriorated. But even had Thibaw been as wise a king as Mindon it would have made little difference to the immediate subsequent history of Burma. British colonial expansion in Burma had only temporarily halted in 1853. The intention to take the rest of the country was ever-present; all that was required was a suitable opportunity, that is to say one which would make it seem that the Burmese and not the British were the trouble-makers. Thibaw provided one before long. Maladministration of his kingdom led to depletion of resources. One of the directions from which funds might be obtained, it seemed to Thibaw, was the British Bombay-Burma Trading Corporation, which had gained a virtual monopoly of timber trading rights in Burma. Thibaw asked the corporation for a loan of a quarter of a million pounds. The corporation refused the loan, for the time was now ripe for British annexation of the remaining Burmese territory. The confusion surrounding the death of Mindon and the accession of Thibaw might have been the occasion for this, for British merchants in Rangoon had been urging it for some time. But at that juncture in affairs it was impossible, for the British army was already fully extended in other places, subduing both the Afghans and the Zulus, as it happened. There was a limit to the number of troops which imperial Britain could put into the field at any one time, and Afghans and Zulus had to be dealt with first; the Burmese could be dealt with later. As a British official resident in Burma at the time wrote, 'had there not been pressing affairs else-where we should doubtless then [in 1879] have occupied Mandalay' (122:35). But six years later it was a different matter. In the pursuit of his unwise policy 'not only did Thibaw simply ask for trouble', wrote G. E. Harvey, 'he chose the very moment when we were in a position to see that he got it' (32:22). So the corporation, provocatively, refused the loan. The Burmese High Court thereupon fined them the exact amount of the requested loan. It was intolerable, as the Viceroy of India, Lord Lytton, wrote in 1878, to have British interests in Burma constantly interfered with by the Burmese. The time had come to put an end to such interference from people who were so inefficient that they could not run their own country. So in 1885 British troops marched into the Burmese king's territory; the king was made 'a prisoner in his palace at Mandalay, under a guard of British infantry. And that', records Harvey, 'was the end of the Burmese kingdom.'

The Burmese Buddhist people stood in crowds in the streets of Mandalay and wept as Thibaw was led away by British troops into captivity; meanwhile Christian Britain had gained great material resources. A British administrator of that period described it in these words: 'As the whole area of Burma was annexed on

January 1st, 1886, all the vast forest wealth it contained was taken over by the British, and the province of Burma forms the great natural storehouse of teak from which the whole world's requirements of this invaluable timber is mainly supplied at present' (74:11, 48).

Burmese Buddhism after the fall of Mandalay

The Burmese saw the annexation not, as British merchants did, in economic terms, but rather as the destruction of their religion and culture. Thibaw's last appeal to them in 1885 had been to resist the English barbarians who had made harsh demands calculated to bring about the destruction of Burma's religion, the violation of national traditions, and the degradation of the race (91:41). The Burmese people agreed with this assessment; when Thibaw was taken through Mandalay in a common cart, surrounded by British redcoats, while 'many women threw themselves into the dust, lamented and wailed, the men left the city carrying all the arms they could find' (37:264). A new era of violence and crime in Burma had been ushered in.

From 1886 onwards there followed for the British occupying forces a far more trying task than that of the easy capture of Mandalay, namely the bringing of the Burmese into submission. This was called by Sir Charles Crosthwaite, who supervised it, the 'pacification of Burma' (18). Not surprisingly, it was a period of considerable religious disorder and indiscipline so far as the Sangha was concerned. Some monks, whom Cady (13:134) calls 'the genuinely pious *pongyis*', assisted in the pacification; others took part in the rebellions that continued for over a decade, but it is open to question whether in Burmese eyes this offering of resistance by monks to foreign rule can be regarded, as Cady regards it, as constituting 'an overt demonstration of religious decay' (13:169). Moreover, as he points out, after 1891 Buddhist ecclesiastical authority was virtually destroyed, 'when a secular judge overruled a disciplinary decision of the Sangha'. One can hardly hold Buddhist monks responsible for cultural dislocations caused by alien British judges whose very presence in Burma it would be difficult to justify from any civilised code of laws. In the course of the 'pacification', patriotic resisters were executed; the occupying power ordered the villages of such resisters to be burned down and prohibited the rebuilding of them. A poem written by one Englishman who felt a deep sense of shame at such atrocities, Major Conway Poole, is quoted by Maung Htin Aung. It describes the hanging of a Burmese village headman on a tree outside his village, and even more ironically portrays Burmese children at the pagoda praying 'that the seeds of Western culture may take root in Eastern lands!' It is understandable that in the years since 1885 many Burmans have not been over-enthusiastic towards Western culture.

The nature of the crisis which the Burmese people experienced in 1885 was, strictly, national and psychological rather than religious. There is evidence that religious belief, practices and institutions continued very much as before, outside the capital city. Bode records that 'the changes brought about in Burma by the annexation . . . affected the Buddhist religion and the Order very little', and quotes Fielding Hall's testimony that, while the monks of Burma ceased to have the direct influence upon public affairs which some of them had exerted before 1885, nevertheless in general the status and prestige of the monks among the people was by no means lessened, 'and of their literary activity we have abundant evidence' (7:94). Commenting on the condition of what he calls 'the elusive Sangha majority' in Burma in 1885 Mendelson suggests that this overwhelming 'passive' majority (politically and sociologically passive, that is) was not much affected by the change of government. It was, he says, 'elusive in so far as it lacked a high degree of organization and leadership and elusive also in that it had a great turnover of personnel'. Moreover, he adds, 'in its very nature, the Sangha is a body which simply does not need self-government, or government of any kind . . . Its simple strength, residing in the patron-monk relationship, still enables a great number of monks to survive today in the way in which it appears the Buddha once wished them to survive' (6:502).

One aspect of the British annexation of 1885 which has received some attention in connection with Buddhist religion in Burma is the failure to appoint a new *thathanabaing*, in the way that Burmese kings had done. This, it is sometimes argued, had a serious, adverse effect on the condition of Burmese Buddhism. Various comments on this argument can be made.

In the first place the influence and power of the *thathanabaing* was already in decline by 1866, for we have Bigandet's evidence to that effect. 'In our days [i.e. at the time of writing], the power of the *thathanabaing* is merely nominal; the effects of his jurisdiction are scarcely felt beyond his own neighbourhood. Such, however, was not the case in former times.' (6:502) When eighteenth-century accounts of the power and activities of the *thathanabaing* are compared with those of the nineteenth century the general impression conveyed by the comparison is that by the latter period the power and importance of the *thathanabaing* was in decline (66: 70).

The British administrators of Burma from 1885 onwards were not unwilling to appoint a successor to the *thathanabaing* of the last Burmese king. The difficulty in doing so lay in the fact that they misunderstood the nature of the task which had devolved upon them. An account of the events of the period written by a British administrator, Sir Henry Thirkell White, records that the Chief Commissioner recognised the importance of enlisting the support of the *thathanabaing* and of offering him whatever help and encouragement it was open to the new government to give, in order to maintain the traditional system:

> At the time of the annexation the *Thathanabaing* was a weak but well-meaning person who had been King Thibaw's tutor. The Chief Commissioner interviewed him in person and essayed to excite his enthusiasm for the new Government . . . The Thathanabaing was induced to visit Rangoon with a view to the extension of his authority over Lower Burma. Government provided for his journey, which was made in some state with a long train of monks. He was received with rapture at Prome and in Rangoon; and a rest-house (Zayat) for him and his successors was built on the slope of the Shwe Dagon Pagoda.

In spite of all that could be done, however, the result only emphasised the extent to which ecclesiastical power had declined in lower Burma between 1852 and 1885, when many of the more ecclesiastical monks had fled from the British-controlled area to the security of Mandalay. 'The effort (by the Chief Commissioner) was ineffectual. Neither that Thathanabaing nor his successors have exercised any power in lower Burma, which still remains in a state of reprobation . . . The Thathanabaing had not the authority, even if he had the will, to control and direct his monks by moral force alone' (122: 188).

When this *thathanabaing* died the problem of appointing a successor faced the government. Not wishing to take the positive action of naming a successor, which would have been contrary to what had become the British policy of neutrality in matters of religion, the government indicated that it would be willing fully to *recognise* any successor whom the Buddhist leaders might wish to name. But this was not the way things had been done by the kings. The chief monks of the Sangha would inevitably disagree, it seems, about whose name should be put forward. The kings had always *declared* who was thathanabaing. As one of the chief monks said, 'What was the use of the Uparaja [vice-regent] asking *us* to decide who shall be Thathanabaing? The pupils of each great Thera will always think it to be wrong to vote for anyone else than his own teacher, and all the Theras will never agree. If the Uparaja, like our Burmese kings, had said, "So and so is the Thathanabaing" then we should accept his selection and everyone would be very pleased' (66: 183).

If there was a single major factor in the change which occurred in the political status and influence of the Sasana during the British period it was not in the absence of a thathanabaing but the absence of a king. The traditional ecclesiastical Buddhism at the pre-1885 days rested heavily on the presence and power of the king, the reflection of whose glory was seen in his thathanabaing. The British conquest, the exiling of the king, and the removal of the royal throne from Mandalay Palace to a museum in Calcutta meant for many Burmese Buddhists the collapse of a cosmology and the system of morality that was largely associated with it. It was this national psychological crisis which was one of the most potent causes of the social and moral upheaval of the period following 1885.

Another crucial factor was the change brought about in the nature of the education which now replaced the traditional, monastery-centred schooling which village boys and girls had received in the old days. At the beginning of the first Anglo-Burmese war, Burma had a higher rate of literacy than England, thanks to the monk-teachers in every village. And at the same time that they learnt to read and write, Burmese children had also absorbed the attitudes and values of their religion. When the new government began to set up schools the education offered was, as Thirkell-White records, 'rigidly secular'. Commenting on this, he says:

It is now felt by many that this policy, however well intentioned, was mistaken, that in allowing, or even encouraging education to be exclusively secular, government had done much to sap the foundations of morality and loyalty, to undermine the basis of character. Probably the right course would have been not to stand aloof from the diverse creeds of the Empire, but to take an active interest in all, and to see that each had fair play and encouragement (122:188).

But such a policy, so far as the Indian Empire was concerned, had to wait until the establishment of the 'secular', or religiously plural independent republic of India in 1947. Any attempt by the British Government of Burma to pursue a policy of this sort would, observed Thirkell White, not have been tolerated by Christian public opinion in England. In words that are well worth recalling, for they have not entirely lost their force, he observed: 'So far as India is concerned the tiresome thing about public opinion in England is that, where interest might be beneficial, it cannot be roused; while in some vital matter in which only the man on the spot has materials for judging, the British public, or its spokesmen, insist on interfering' (122:188).

With the establishment of British rule in Burma, forms of employment were being offered in Rangoon and other towns, in commercial and government offices, for which the traditional education – namely reading, writing, and study of the scriptures – was not an appropriate preparation. Burmese Buddhist parents began sending their children to missionary and government schools. The devaluation of monastic education resulted in a reduction in the amount of religious and moral instruction being given to the young, and predisposed them to look down on the excessively traditionalist learning of the monks. On the other hand, the new style of education had consequences for Burma which Protestant missionaries may not have foreseen: it produced a new type of Buddhist layman, who was able to bring to bear upon the hitherto excessively text-centred religious teaching of the monks something of a wider world. However, had the monks in village monastery schools been given adequate opportunities and encouragement it is possible that they might have co-operated in expanding the scope of village education. A British memorandum of 1868–9 had already recognised this possibility. It noted that 'the best method for reaching the masses in British Burma' was the village monastery- school. It proposed that books dealing with subjects such as arithmetic and land measuring should be made available to the village schools. If these 'were furnished to the Chief *Phongyee* of each Monastery, and a qualified Burmese teacher engaged to superintend the studies occasionally' then it was likely 'that the books supplied would be willingly used' (45:89). Had such a policy of co-operation with Buddhist monks at village level in the work of education been vigorously followed, it might well have prevented the alienation of many Burmese children from Buddhist religion and culture, and there might have been a significantly different sequel to British rule in Burma. But the general policy towards Buddhism which was forced upon British administrators by the religious arrogance of some nineteenth-century Englishmen, and the pursuit of money which began under British rule, together ensured that Buddhist monastery education declined. Moreover, in the event, many monks were unwilling to co-operate.

The subject is a large one, and hasty generalisations in such a complex area are dangerous, but perhaps a tentative conclusion may be suggested at this point. In the case of British *political* irruption into the life of Burma it was mainly the ecclesiastical form of Buddhism, (that is the sasana, which flourished under the patronage of kings) which suffered, because of the extent to which royal power was, so to speak, its life-blood; other, local forms, the 'passive' or Vinaya-ruled and Vinaya-following Sanghas, would not have been greatly affected by political interference. But in the case of British *educational* irruption into the national life of Burma it was the entire fabric of Burmese Buddhist religion that suffered; the damage was more widespread, and was felt in thousands of villages and towns throughout Buddhist Burma. R. Grant Brown, who worked in Burma for twenty-eight years from 1889, opens his account of education there by pointing to 'the remarkable fact that the Burmese had universal education of a sort long before anything of the kind existed in any European country' (9:90). He ends his account with the sad observation that British educational policy in Burma had brought about a reversal of that earlier, happier condition of things:

> What it has done is to equip, or attempt to equip, with knowledge the children of a tiny group of people who happened to have money or to live in Rangoon. As a result we have a handful of Burmans who are both educated and intelligent, a great many who are educated but not intelligent, and a great many more (sc. outside Rangoon) who are intelligent but not educated (9:100).

The Thai state and religious nonconformity

In the hills of northern Thailand, remote from the capital city of Bangkok, there existed until the end of the nineteenth century two virtually independent kingdoms. In those days they did not regard themselves as 'Siamese' in the sense in which the court of Bangkok did, and in the sense which the people of the central plain of Thailand were expected to do. The people of the northern hills had more in common with the Shans of what are now the Shan States of Burma, just across the border, and with the people of Laos, and to some extent the people of southern China. In that hilly region which now forms part of Thailand there were two small kingdoms, namely Chiengmai and Nan. The people of these two kingdoms were Buddhists, but they used a different script for their sacred books, they observed different rituals, and the organisation of their monkhood, the Sangha, was different. The type of Buddhist religion they followed has been called the 'Yuan' cult (22:75).

The organisation of the Buddhist monks in this area was much less centralised and much less authoritarian than that of central Thailand, dominated as the plain was by Bangkok. Here, by contrast, each monastery was more or less independent of any external control, ordination of new monks was in the hands of the abbot of each monastery, and each monastery was supported by the local people. Some of the people were Buddhist supporters, and many were tribal people following their own religion (46: 552).

By the end of the nineteenth century, however, the local political autonomy of the northern kingdoms had disappeared. Pressure from colonial powers, the British in Burma to the west, and the French in Indo-China to the east, had forced the king of Siam to look to the frontiers of his territory and to guard the extent of his kingdom. He took steps to strengthen the authority of Bangkok over as wide an area as he could between these two empire-hungry European powers. A Shan uprising in the north in 1901 precipitated a crisis and led to immediate measures being taken not only to control the north more effectively but to incorporate it politically and culturally into the Siamese Kingdom. Its cultural assimilation entailed the incorporation of all the Buddhist monks of the north into the nationally organised Siamese Sangha, controlled from Bangkok. The legal measure which effected this change was the Sangha Administration Act of 1902. This was the first of three such Acts affecting the monks of Thailand. The Act was aimed at controlling and rationalising the structure of the Sangha, as also were the two later Acts, of 1941 and 1963. The 1902 Act laid it down that all monks throughout the

Kingdom of Siam were to form a national Sangha. It provided also for a hierarchical system of discipline, with the seniormost monks in Bangkok exercising control over those immediately below them and so on, and having power to punish monks who were disobedient. It provided also for a nationally organised system of education so that monastic teaching and practice could be standardised throughout the kingdom. This educational system was very largely the work of the supreme patriarch of the Siamese Buddhist Order, Vajiranana, whose work of rationalising the Sangha will be mentioned later. The powers and duties of the abbot of a monastery were clearly defined in the Act, and the appointment of abbots was made a duty of government officials, or could be undertaken by the king personally if he so chose; this latter type of appointment was usually to ecclesiastical posts in Bangkok. The similarity between this system of controlling and imposing uniformity on a variety of local religious communities and the system which operates in a state church in a European country is remarkably close. There is also a clear reflection, in the titles, grades and ranks, and in the concentration of the highest titles in Bangkok, of the system of political administration. As S. J. Tambiah has commented, 'whatever changes have taken place in later times in the details of ecclesiastical organisation, the fundamental features of the Sangha hierarchy and its relation to political authority were molded in 1902 and have not changed up to the present time' (102:238).

The intention of the system which was thus brought into being was the enforcement over the whole country of a national standard of orthodoxy laid down by Bangkok, and thus the prevention of any possible regional religious autonomy or independence which might lend strength to regional political autonomy. The Buddhist Sangha was, in other words, being forged into an instrument of the Thai state. The Bangkok style of Buddhist practice and organisation was being set up as the standard, 'true' and orthodox form, with the implication that standardisation was a noble, pious and praiseworthy activity; and resistance to it was reprehensible and wicked. This has continued to be the tendency in Thai Buddhist development, and it provides an interesting example, among a number of others, of the effect upon a religious tradition of its becoming politicised.

4

The Growth of Nationalism: 1900–1945

Innovations in Burmese Buddhism, 1900–1910

By the turn of the century, certain Buddhist innovations were beginning to appear in Burma. In the years immediately before and after 1900 a number of religious-cultural associations were formed in Moulmein, Mandalay and Bassein. In 1897 some educated Buddhist laymen in the Moulmein area founded the Sasanadara Society, for the purpose of promoting social and educational reforms. They started a high school with a Western type of curriculum, with laymen rather than monks as teachers, using both English and Burmese languages. Their modernistic attitude is further illustrated by the fact that the funds for their venture were to come from the savings which would be made by cutting down expenditure on traditional Burmese social ceremonies such as funerals, weddings, ordinations, and ear-borings. Soon afterwards, a similar association in Mandalay, the Buddha Kalayama Meikta Athin, set up a lay school where Buddhist religion was taught and the Buddhist lunar holy days (sometimes in English called 'Sabbaths') were observed. Another such society was founded in Bassein, in the delta; it was named the Ashoka Society after the English monk who helped to start it. This man, whose original name was Gordon Douglas, 'a person of high social standing in England . . . son of a well-known Earl . . . was said to have come to the East owing to his being an out and out radical with socialistic tendencies' (42, IX, 1, 1900: 3).

The ordinary Burmese monks had little or no interest in activities of this kind; many regarded them with deep suspicion.

Monastic education was limited to traditional subjects. The establishment of Christian missionary and government schools had caused the Burmese laymen who had attended them to look upon the traditional learning of the monasteries as inadequate as a programme of education in the twentieth century. But the monks in the main had no knowledge of anything other than traditional subjects, and were 'above all advice', so far as non-traditional education was concerned; some, the more strict, banned such subjects as modern geography (which conflicted with the traditional, India-derived geography in which Mount Meru was the centre of the universe) and arithmetic as sinful (13:179).

The Burmese Buddhist revival of this period, therefore, was largely a lay movement. Another of its manifestations was the Young Men's Buddhist Association (YMBA). This was to some extent the successor of the earlier lay Buddhist associations in Moulmein, Mandalay, and Bassein which have already been mentioned. The idea of such an association had its roots also in Ceylon, where a YMBA had been in existence since 1898. This was part of the process, amounting almost to mimicry, by which Sinhalese Buddhists attempted to show that point for point their religion was at least the equal of the Protestant religion of the British rulers of the island. For Burma, as a neighbouring Buddhist country experiencing the same alien rule, it was appropriate to adopt similar devices for giving vent to similar national religious feelings, and the formation of a YMBA was one of them. The first such association in Burma was formed in the Arakan in 1902, with a headquarters and student hostel and a code of discipline (42, March 1902: 102). Another, and subsequently more influential, YMBA was founded in Rangoon in 1906. A common feature of the independence struggle in colonial territories in Asia in the late nineteenth and early twentieth centuries was the use of religious organisations and institutions as the vehicles for early forms of protest against imperial rule. For this was one of the few available ways of expressing dissent from the attitudes, assumptions, and cultural norms of the occupying power. It was a relatively safe form of protest because it was not overtly political; such dissent could be represented as nothing more than the affirming of traditional religion; it was the one relatively autonomous area of life left to colonial peoples. Relatively, but not entirely, for some of the occasions for protest were that religion had been interfered with. It was possible to protest on these grounds, however, where it would not have been possible to protest on political grounds. The general principle which British colonial rulers had learnt to adopt was that as far as possible the religion of conquered peoples should not be interfered with. The YMBA was, at the outset, to all intents and purposes a religious organisation, an attempt to give Buddhism a form and an expression that would be consonant with Western learning. The small minority of Western-educated Burmese who founded it were making the 'tacit admission that little creative adjustment to the cultural impact of the outside world could be expected from the traditionalist and declining Buddhist Sangha' (13:179). The monastery schools with their exclusively traditional teaching were by 1910 already losing ground to the lay schools. In 1891 there had been 4,324 government-recognised monastic schools and only 890 lay schools. In 1897 the numbers were, respectively, 3,281 and 1,216. By 1910 the lay schools had gained the lead; there were 2,653 of these and only 2,208 monastic schools. Seven years later the gap had widened to 4,650 lay to 2,977 monastic schools. These figures are a significant indication of a national trend, since half of Burma's children between the ages of six and fifteen who received any schooling at all were enrolled in these 7,627 schools. The fact that the majority were in lay rather than monastic schools is evidence of the general trend, a trend which could already be seen by 1900. Cady observes that the educational function of the monks decreased in importance after 1900 and the traditional role of the monasteries in nurturing Burmese children in Buddhist religious belief and practice began to be lost. Moreover, the displacement of monastic education 'not only reduced the amount of religious and moral instruction imparted to the youth but also discredited in the eyes of the educated elite the prescientific lore of the pongyis' (13: 170f).

This was undoubtedly one of the factors responsible for the founding of the YMBAs. They were in their early period *religious* associations; they existed for the promotion of Buddhist ways of thought and action more relevant to the twentieth century. U Ba Maw, whose boyhood years these were, recalls that the YMBAs 'were formed in a few big towns after the pattern of the Christian YMCAs. Their name itself shows that religion was their chief concern . . .' (4:7). Their organisers included U May Oung, a Cambridge graduate, U Kin, a man who later accepted British knighthood, and other future national leaders. By 1910 the Rangoon YMBA had fifteen affiliated branches in such towns as Moulmein, Bassein, Pegu, Prome and Mandalay. The Associations were, as we shall see, destined to play an increasingly political role after 1910, but at first they existed primarily and indeed almost exclusively as religious organisations. Their subsequent history demonstrates the way in which something that begins as a religious and non-political phenomenon can, in certain circumstances, be fairly quickly pressed into the service of politics. One organisation in particular remained thoroughly Buddhist in character. This was the Buddhist Propaganda Society, founded in 1908. 'By 1909 it claimed to have 1,210 members and eight monks engaged in preaching. A frankly proselytizing society engaged in the propagation of Buddhism, it never became a mass organisation . . .' (114:8).

Not all the Buddhist monks were of the rigidly traditionalist kind, nor were they all ill disciplined, although by this time, with the lengthening history of the Sangha's degeneration under British rule, many of them were. Here and there some outstanding exceptions were to be found. One or two of the more prominent of these had a great influence on the already awakened laymen. The writing and preaching of the abbot known as the Ledi Sayadaw is perhaps the most notable. Himself a very learned monk, he 'made the scriptures accessible to the people by retelling the stories from the life of the Buddha in simple but effective verses, which little children could easily learn or recite . . . He encouraged villagers to form small religious groups to go around the village reciting his verses or simpler texts from the scriptures and discussing some of the main teachings of Buddhism' (37). At the scholarly level his work was known and admired in other Theravada Buddhist countries, and a Western scholar has compared his Pali writings to the great tradition of Burmese Pali literature of the twelfth century, consisting as they do of a Pali grammar; a discourse on *nibbana*; a treatise on meditation; stanzas for recitation as charms; an exposition of the law; an exposition of the Eightfold Path; a manual of Abhidhamma; and various other works of a teaching and expository nature (7: 97f). His preaching and writing had a direct influence on the thought and ideology of the Thakin movement which became one of the important elements of Burmese nationalism a decade or so later.

Burma: from religious revival to nationalism

In Burma as in other colonial territories in Asia religion provided the leaders, the techniques and the ideology by means of which the emerging nationalist movement sought to rid the country of alien rule (95:95f). Both elements of Burmese Buddhism, the modernist and the traditional, the YMBA and the monks, developed into sources of energy for the nationalist struggle.

We have seen that the YMBA was in origin the expression of a concern among educated Burmans to reinterpret and re-express Buddhism in contemporary terms; both their intention and their achievement justify the use of the expression 'Buddhist revival' to characterise the significance of the movement. In a country where adherence to Buddhism was regarded as the main criterion of national identity ('To be Burman is to be Buddhist') the revival of Buddhism necessarily meant the revival of Burman national consciousness. It was in the activities of the YMBA from 1916 onwards that the first clear signs of organised resistance to British rule were seen. At the meeting of the General Council of Young Men's Buddhist Associations in 1916 a number of younger delegates, recently returned from higher education in India and Europe, tried to persuade the rest of the members to widen the Associations' field of interest to include political matters. Although they were unsuccessful in this attempt, a practical issue was taken up shortly afterwards by all the Associations, which, although overtly a religious affair, had strong nationalistic political implications. This was the controversy over the wearing of shoes at Buddhist pagodas. The normal custom in the Buddhist countries of South–East Asia is for a person to remove his or her shoes at the entrance to a pagoda and walk barefoot within the pagoda area. The same is done when entering an ordinary house. When the British came out of interest or curiosity to visit pagodas such as the magnificent Shwe Dagon pagoda in Rangoon, they objected to performing this courtesy. Edwardian Englishmen and Englishwomen considered it an affront to their dignity in some way, or perhaps they were afraid of disease. It meant also an admission that there was one area in Burma where they could not do exactly as they liked. If the British really were afraid they might contract some disease from visiting a Buddhist pagoda and objected to following the usage necessary to respect the religious feelings of those whose shrine it was, clearly they could have stayed away. That they were not prepared to follow this more discreet course and preferred to insist on their alleged right to tramp round a shrine in their outdoor shoes led to a controversy into which the YMBAs threw themselves with great vigour. The matter had been raised once or twice before; under the leadership of a Burmese barrister, U Theing Maung, it was taken up with a sudden new vigour in 1916 and 1917. About fifty branches of the YMBA gave strong support to the opposition to British practice in this matter and thus became united in what was overtly a Buddhist cause, but which became also the focus of anti-British nationalist feelings. In 1918, in the interest of public tranquillity the government had to order a 'closure on public discussion' and ruled that the head monk at each local pagoda should decide what the requirements were to be with regard to footwear' (67:24). The British inhabitants of Rangoon thereupon decided that if they had to visit the Shwe Dagon pagoda shoeless they would not visit it at all, and persisted in depriving themselves in this way until after the Second World War.

Burmese nationalism gathers strength

In 1917 the British Government, through Edwin Montagu, the Secretary of State for India, issued a policy statement which acknowledged the need for developing self-governing institutions *in India*. Nothing was said concerning Burma. The YMBA in Burma responded to this by sending a delegation to Calcutta in December 1917 to remind Montagu and the Viceroy, Lord Chelmsford, of Burma's existence, and of the similar self-governing aspirations of its people. In April 1918 the Montagu-Chelmsford report, referring to Burma's political development, simply set the matter aside 'for separate consideration in the future' (67:25). The YMBA thereupon decided to bring Burma's case directly to the British Parliament, and, together with other associated organisations, raised £2,000 to send a three-man deputation. The three arrived in London in 1919 and the outcome of the negotiations, which do not concern us here, was certain mild concessions on paper. This appeared to be the sum total of interest in the matter which the British in London were prepared to show; the result was growing dissatisfaction in Burma. In 1920 the YMBA organised various forms of protest – a boycott on elections of Burmese members to the Indian Parliament in Delhi, and a student boycott on the new Rangoon University, which had been established that year.

Just as modern Buddhist organisations were providing the leadership and the resources for the nationalist movement in the towns and cities, some members of the traditional Buddhist institution, the Sangha, were beginning to do the same in the villages. One of the first monks to be involved was U Ottama, who in 1921 returned to Burma from India (where he had been a left-wing member of the Indian National Congress party) to travel about the country preaching the necessity of self-rule for Burma. He urged the monks, in the defence of Buddhism, to leave their monasteries and to take up the nationalist struggle. By the more conservative members of the Sangha he was rejected, largely because of his political activities but also because of his infringements of the canonical code of conduct for monks. Nevertheless he gained a following among younger monks in his continuing campaign, until this was brought to an end temporarily by the colonial government. U Ottama was arrested, charged with seditious activities, and sentenced to ten months imprisonment. This greatly enhanced his influence. When he was released in 1922 he was able to take up the campaign again with renewed success, so that his radicalism spread like wildfire and disaffection was kept at fever pitch (89:30). Once again he was arrested and imprisoned, this time for three years. The pattern was repeated, until at last he died in prison in 1939. Cady comments that 'U Ottama did for nationalism in Burma part of what Gandhi did for it in India by transforming an essentially political problem into a religious one' (13:232). However, an important difference was that Gandhi and the Congress party were able to find their major support among the middle classes and business community, whereas the Burmese nationalist leaders, having no middle classes to support them, had to turn to the politically activated monks and the villagers. By 1924 organisations known as *wunthanu athins* (nationalist associations) were to be found in almost every village in Burma (67:33). Moreover, the YMBA had by the early 1920s been succeeded by a more comprehensive organisation called the General Council of Burmese Associations (GCBA), which directed the activities of the village-based nationalist *athins*. These, too, had arisen originally out of a popular desire to see Burmese life purged of the corruption, drunkenness and crime into which it had fallen during the period of British rule, and restored to good order, with a reformed Sangha able to take the lead in promoting moral and social welfare. In the course of a few years, however, they became increasingly agencies of political agitation (13:234f), much of which, especially after about 1921, was encouraged by politically inclined monks, who 'led political protest but were not prepared to offer anything new to their people except a return to pre-colonial norms'. They 'played a dominant role in submerging the real issues of the day in a miasma of protest and agitation at the local level,' comments Satyamurthy, 'and by pushing to the sidelines essential questions relating to the development of a modern nationalistic ideology suitable to Burma . . .' (89: 29, 31). In Satyamurthy's view the perpetual unrest which these political *pongyis* generated had the effect of blocking the efforts of more responsible leaders to find an authentic new national identity for the Burma of the twentieth century, and did greater damage to the efforts of Burma to achieve national unity than any other single force.

A prominent feature of the anti-foreign spirit engendered by some of these monks was the presentation of nationalistic aspirations in terms of Buddhist religious ideas. Freedom from bondage and progress towards nirvana was interpreted by the Sayadaw U Thilasara in 1923 to mean freedom from *political* bondage. Independence for Burma was to mean nirvana within this world, and was to be attained by means of political struggle, according to another popular preacher, Sayadaw U Nye Ya (86: 126).

Saya San's bid for kingship

One of the most famous examples of a blending of popular Burmese mythology, nationalism and traditional royalism was seen in the uprising known as the Saya San rebellion which began in 1930. By that time, forty-five years had passed since Burma ceased to be a Buddhist kingdom – long enough for monks to learn to resent their increasingly inferior status in British-ruled India and long enough for the memory of Burma's kings to have become invested with a glow of nostalgic romance. The hope of bringing British rule to an end was expressed in terms of the hope of restoring Burmese kingship. The two events were thought of as closely connected; the revival of the institution of kingship might well be the occasion, so it was believed, for the overthrow of foreign imperial rule. From 1910 onwards there were a number of abortive rebellions combining these two aims (13:310).

The rebellion of Saya San began in December, 1930 in Tharrawaddy District, in lower Burma. The Shan chieftains were invited to support Saya San's 'ardent desire to advance religion and the nation'. Formerly Saya San had been a monk, but for the past few years he had instead been working in a more directly political role. His movement had a strongly traditional Burmese religious aura. Most of his principal supporters were political monks associated with local nationalist *athins*, and his 'coronation', which took place at his jungle capital, at a time and on a day declared auspicious by the astrologers, (11.30 p.m. on 28 October 1930) was carried out in a thoroughly traditional Burmese religious manner. In a symbolically cosmocentric royal 'palace', of bamboo decorated with tinsel, he was declared to be the *Galon*, the mythical bird who would destroy the *Naga*, the snake, or foreigner. He was surrounded by magicians with their bodies tattooed with *galon* figures (for invulnerability) and who were armed with the full range of protective medicines, amulets, charms, and guardian spirits. The great Nats (guardian spirits) and the lesser Nats were invoked in a solemn oath and prayer. To these Burmese religious elements of the occasion there was added the Brahman symbol of divine kingship, the White Umbrella, which was raised over the new king's head, together with the crown and sword, and the sacred slippers.

As with the traditional Burmese kings of the old days, so with this new 'king', there was not much that was specifically Buddhist in the symbolism in which his kingship was expressed. An 'army' was then gathered, drilled and indoctrinated, and on 22 December the rebellion was launched. It was soon declared to be a problem the police could not handle, and British troops were deployed in the areas to which it had now spread; they were aided by Karen irregulars and volunteers. According to Moscotti 'the *pongyis* were instrumental in the spread of the rebellion through much of Lower Burma and the Shan States' (67:58f). On the other hand, G. E. Harvey, of the Indian Civil Service in Burma, records that 'none of the minority races [which would include the Shans] joined it; indeed they supplied us with auxiliary troops'. Apart from this, he says, the Burmese people were divided. If they had sympathised with the rebellion, they soon came to dread it. The government had a little help from a timid public,' he adds, 'and from the Buddhist clergy' (32:75). These two accounts can be seen to confirm what appears from other evidence, namely that the Buddhist Sangha and people were divided in the degree of their support of political, and especially violent political, struggle. After the rebellion had been brought to an end in August 1931, some monks formed 'peace missions' to visit the villages which had been affected by the disturbance and to help restore a calmer atmosphere (67:60). What the outbreak and the course of the rebellion did reveal was the extent to which nationalism was rooted in Burmese tradition but made use of Buddhist institutions when it was appropriate and profitable to do so. It revealed also how the Buddhist Sangha was divided between those who were more and those who were less inclined to Burmese tradition. Some of the laymen who had taken part in the rebellion saw their own action in a Buddhist perspective, after the event. For example, one chieftain, Bo Hla Maung, having surrendered and knowing what his fate would be, 'replied that his cause was lost, and all his relatives taken by the British' but that 'by his surrender they would be freed', and, as for himself, he remained 'steadfast in his faith, in the justice of fate and in the path that leads at last to Nirvana, of the wheel that swings immutably through many lives, not deviating a hair's breadth from its track, until men are loosened from it for everlasting peace' (118:96). Other Buddhists could have offered other interpretations of how Bo Hla Maung's actions were likely to have affected his future progress on the path.

The rebellion finally ran out into banditry and the terrorisation of village people. Saya San was captured in the Shan States, near Maymyo, and handed over to the government. It is noteworthy that it was in Shan territory that he was handed over; the Shans, although mainly Buddhist, had shown little enthusiasm for the rebellion; the Karens had taken part in the pacification; and the whole movement had had a characteristically traditional *Burmese* appearance. Maung Htin Aung, writing from a strongly Burmese point of view, glorifies the rebellion, and evaluates it as 'the nearest Asian counterpart of the peasants' rebellion in medieval England' (37:292). The close approximation between what is Burmese and what is 'Burmese Buddhist' has to be borne in mind here; some Burmese Buddhists have claimed that the two terms are virtually equivalent. Whether or not in the eyes of the purist 'Burmese Buddhism' is quite the same as 'Buddhism' makes no difference in real situations in Burma. To the Karen the Burmese king, whether a king in fact or, like Saya San, by ambition only, was the promoter of Buddhism.

Burmese xenophobia

Burmese nationalism during the 1930s was fed from various sources. One was the presence of alien groups whose attitudes inevitably caused them to be regarded as usurpers of the rights of the Burmese, and a threat to them in their own country. The British were obviously the prime case of this sort; the Indians in Burma were another. In 1930 riots broke out in Rangoon as a consequence of a clash between Indian and Burmese dock labourers. Accumulated resentment against Indians, especially on account of their entrepreneurial moneymaking activities, burst out into violence in which there was strong consciousness of national identities. It was the occasion for Burmese people to emphasise specifically Burmese characteristics. They got themselves tattooed by the many *sayas* who were there to meet the demand, and decorated with various traditional Burmese charms they roved the streets of Rangoon in mobs, hunting Indians and killing hundreds of them (13:305). The Burmese, who had been forced to feel their inferiority, felt they were at last masters again. Maurice Collis, who was in Burma at the time, records the feeling of the Burmese that 'nearly all the rich people in the country were foreigners' and that 'all sorts of foreigners lorded it over them' (17:215).

Another form which anti-foreign feeling took was opposition by the more politically orientated monks to the teaching of Christianity to Buddhist children in missionary schools. It was not until 1938, however, that this resentment of foreigners, expressed in terms of religious differences, took a violent public form. The conflict on this occasion was, in Ba Maw's words, 'between the Buddhists, who were Burmese, and the Muslims, who were mainly Indians' (4:13). The pretext was Muslim offensiveness towards Buddhism. A book originally published in 1931, without causing trouble, had reappeared in 1937, when it provided a convenient excuse for political opportunists to instigate violent action. 'A few objectionable comments in a tract written by an utterly unimportant Muslim set off the first sparks, but it became a really serious conflagration,' wrote Ba Maw, who was Prime Minister at that time (4:13), and whose government the opportunists were deliberately seeking to wreck. In outward appearance, however, it was contrived so as to look like a religious conflict. The vernacular press published quotations from the offending book, maligning Buddhism; to these were joined accusations against Muslims who took Burmese (Buddhist) wives and maligned their religion. A mass meeting of political monks was held in the precincts of the Shwe Dagon pagoda, on 26 July, 1938, a procession was organised, going from the pagoda through the city to the Indian quarter, where it became a mob seeking vengeance on Muslim Indians. Within a few days the whole Rangoon area was affected by anti-Indian hysteria, and it was some time before law and order was restored. Some words about religion had served as the spark, but long stored-up grievances against foreigners, in this case Indians, provided the vast resources of fuel which fed the fire. It was not in any basic sense a conflict of Buddhists versus Muslims but one of Burmese versus foreigners. Burmese nationalism can be seen to be negative as well as positive: the rejection of foreign interference in the life of the country, as well as the affirming of a sense of Burmese cultural identity.

Towards the rationalisation of the Thai Sangha

In contrast to Burma, where in the modern period the Sangha has maintained a lively diversity and certainly cannot be accused of having fallen into dull uniformity, whether of ideas or organisation, in Thailand the trend has throughout the twentieth century been one of increasing centralisation and the imposition of unity from above. The policy of rationalising the Sangha gradually gathered strength during the Bangkok era, especially from the time of King Mongkut (Rama IV). It was successfully continued by a son of Mongkut named Vajiranana, who was the abbot of Wat Bovorn in Bangkok and, from 1910, Supreme Patriarch of Thailand. Under his influence the Sangha was not only rationalised; its transformation into a bureaucratic organisation was rapidly advanced. He is said to have been 'a brilliant and capable organiser' (107:641), and has been described as the most celebrated monk in the history of Thailand (19:14). Born in 1860, he became a novice at the age of fourteen and a bhikkhu at the age of twenty. He remained for the rest of his life a member of the Sangha and most of that time he spent in the royal wat in Bangkok. He became head of the Dhammayutika sect in 1906 and was made Supreme Patriarch in 1910.

As abbot of Wat Bovorn, he was, in a number of ways, very like his father and famous predecessor Mongkut. Although he was only eight years old when his father died, Vajiranana had received from Mongkut 'his temper, his intellectual acquisitiveness, his exasperation at the nonchalance of others, and his untiring activity' (53:97). He possessed a similar deep religious conviction combined with the spirit of rational inquiry. He had learnt English as a boy and was familiar with the company of Europeans. In one quality he is said to have differed from his father, namely his love of good order. He regretted what he saw as the untidiness of the division of the Thai Sangha into two sects, the Mahanikaya and the Dhammayutika founded by his father, and would like to have seen the reunion of the two into an undivided Sangha. Although he did not succeed in this ambition, he did achieve a very great deal in other ways in terms of administrative reconstruction of the Sangha and in various educational reforms and innovations.

Buddhist education in Thailand had until then been 'a haphazard affair' (19:17). Each bhikkhu followed his own inclination in what he studied and taught and this resulted in much unevenness in the depth and extent of understanding of essential Buddhist ideas, and of the Pali literature. Vajiranana laid down clearly defined courses of study for monks and for laymen, at two levels. One was an elementary course of Buddhist education, or 'education in Dhamma', using Thai language, for monks who intended to stay only a few months in the Sangha, according to the usual custom for young men in Thailand. The other was an advanced course using Pali language, and was for those monks who intended to remain indefinitely in the Sangha as a religious vocation. The elementary course was offered to laymen also, and in time began to attract increasing numbers of them.

Vajiranana composed textbooks for these courses, and introduced written examinations in place of the exclusively oral method which had been used until then. He wrote very extensively in the Pali language as well as in Thai; his literary output included sermons, translations, commentaries, and works of exposition and popularisation. He travelled extensively throughout the kingdom, ensuring that his educational reforms were properly put into effect, explaining them and persuading monks to whom all this seemed strange and unnecessary just how valuable and important his programme was. He carried out a reorganisation of the wat communities and of their revenue system; the latter produced a marked growth in their income. His efforts eventually had a deep and lasting effect; the methods he introduced 'are still in constant and continuous use all over the country, with only a few innovations needing to be made to follow the changing circumstances of the times' (19:19).

Wat Bovoranives in Bangkok, of which he was the abbot, thus became firmly established as a leading centre of Buddhist education and administration.

Buddhism and Thai nationalism

Again in contrast with Burma, where nationalism had begun to grow naturally by the early years of the twentieth century, in

Thailand it almost had to be forced. It was not that the Thais had no proper national pride; but, not having had their nationhood threatened since the middle of the eighteenth century, and having then survived the threat and grown in strength, they had by the beginning of the twentieth ceased to be self-conscious about nationhood. Moreover, no alien ideology had been able to secure a position of advantage and Buddhism had continued to provide a basis of cultural unity and to exert an influence at all levels of society. However, the time came when a conscious attempt to develop a more lively and militant Thai nationalism was made. This happened during the second and third decades of the twentieth century; it was an attempt made partly in the name of Buddhism, and has had lasting consequences. It may be seen to have begun with the reign of Rama VI.

The coronation of King Vajiravudh, or Rama VI, of Thailand in 1910 was attended by (among other guests) H.I.H. The Grand Duke Boris of Russia. His military attaché, Colonel Grabbé, while he was in Bangkok, was given a rosary by the Supreme Buddhist Patriarch of Thailand. This rosary, so we are told, was specially blessed by His Holiness for the Buddhist Cossacks of the Russian Army. No doubt it was received with due gratitude by the colonel. King Vajiravudh was the kind of Buddhist monarch who approved of such gifts, just as he welcomed such imperial and military guests at his coronation. The Thai king had been trained at Sandhurst Military Academy in England; he had been commissioned as an officer in the Royal Durham Light Infantry, and had later been made an honorary British general. On his return to Thailand he had done his best to arouse in the Thai people two qualities in which he considered they were lamentably lacking, namely a proper national pride and a spirit of military discipline. One of the consequences of his, as it seems, not too popular attempts to instil these qualities into the people was that some ill-disciplined persons tried to assassinate him, unsuccessfully as it happened.

King Vajiravudh (Rama VI) is remembered chiefly for his attempt to increase the spirit of nationalism among the Thai people. His reign, from 1910 to 1925, covered the period of the First World War and the years immediately before and after it. The first Siamese monarch to be educated in the West, he had spent nine years in England, from 1893 to 1902, after which he returned to Siam by way of the U.S.A., visiting President Theodore Roosevelt (with whom he exchanged military reminiscences), and Japan, where he was able to see the rapid modernisation which had taken place during the thirty-four years since the Meiji period began.

With his military background it is perhaps not surprising that he 'tried to play the potentate' (93:139), and that he had the distinction of being the first king of the Bangkok dynasty upon whom an assassination attempt was made on the basis of hostility to his policies. Subsequently he made some concessions in the way of encouraging commoners to play some part in government, enough to enable a high-ranking Thai civil servant later to write in his private diary regarding Vajiravudh that his policy 'favoured not only princes but also common people' (99: 170).

During the eight years he spent in Bangkok after his return from Europe, America and Japan, he came to the conclusion that the Thai people lacked a corporate spirit. Their Buddhism, he said, had no relevance to contemporary life; it was kept going merely by inertia. As a result of this they had become preoccupied with personal salvation, and this had made them individualistic. They were not uniting in common service, and were not making suitable efforts to exploit their national resources (107:636f). How far this was an accurate assessment of the situation so far as Thai Buddhism was concerned is open to question; so also is the appropriateness of his highly special interpretation of Buddhist norms and values when it came to the exploiting of national resources.

On becoming king he embarked on an ambitious programme for making good the deficiency in nationalistic spirit. He founded a military organisation called the Wild Tigers Corps, resembling the British Territorial (i.e. civilian) Army, with a junior organisation for boys called the Tiger Cubs, which was later assimilated to the Boy Scout movement. These both had as their aim the encouragement of loyalty to Nation, Religion and King (an echo of the British trio 'God, King and Country'). He believed that religion had an important part to play in fostering the spirit of nationalism. In the furtherance of this idea, he had the practice of saying Buddhist prayers introduced in various public institutions such as government schools, the police force and the army. He firmly rejected the idea that such practices were inappropriate to Buddhism, and denied that Buddhism was primarily concerned with meditation. He went so far as to say, in his 'sermons' to the Wild Tigers, that Buddhism's positive qualities could best be seen on the battlefields; 'fighting men with a belief in Buddha's teachings would not flee, because their belief in dhamma strengthened their courage and convinced them that the sacrifice of their life was an advantage'. What was more, the Thai people had a Buddhist cause to fight for; in Vajiravudh's view Thailand was the last line of defence for Buddhism now that (as he held) it had been destroyed in almost every other country. If they did not accept their responsibility for Buddhism and fight for it, the Thai people would be ensuring its end (26:257f). He appears to have been taking an excessively gloomy view of the condition of Buddhism in those countries where European colonial rule had affected it and had been, so it was alleged, the cause of its decadence, such as Ceylon, Burma, Laos and Cambodia. His argument seems to assume that Buddhism was to be written off in those countries. If he was being less than realistic on this issue it was because such ideas served the important purpose of stimulating nationalist sentiment. As Thailand was not at war with any of its neighbours at that particular time, he attempted, says Stephen Green, 'to do the next best thing, stimulate the conditions of war' (26:254).

The policy of glorifying military virtues and enhancing the place of the army in Thai national life carried out by Rama VI had long-term consequences which have continued to be felt more than half a century after his death in 1925. The Thai army, built up by the king in the early years of the twentieth century with the declared intention of defending Buddhist civilisation, was by mid-century to become the dominant power in Thailand, and by the last quarter of the century it has become evident that the Buddhist Sangha in Thailand is being required to assist in implementing the policies of the Thai military elite, policies which to some Buddhists are odious.

Thailand's quiet revolution, 1925–1940

The close personal links which existed between the Thai royal family and the Sangha throughout the period of the Bangkok monarchy, from 1782 onwards, meant that there was a very sensitive relationship between the two institutions. There is, however, the other side of the relationship. The kings of Thailand were the kind of kings they were partly at least because they were also Buddhists. In the Bangkok period especially this was because of the close personal relationship and identity of background between the king and the most influential monks. It follows that Buddhism in Thailand is particularly vulnerable to any change in the constitutional pattern. Such a change took place during the reign of the king who succeeded Vajiravudh. This was one of his younger brothers, Prajadhipok, who in 1925, at the age of thirty-two, became Rama VII. Educated in England at Eton College and at a military academy in France, he was perhaps as much at home outside Thailand as within it. Inheriting an enormous debt in the royal accounts from Rama VI, who had been a very big spender, he had difficult political decisions to make on the safest way, internationally and nationally, of reducing it. He appointed three of his uncles and two half-brothers as an advisory Council of State. There were public murmurs because no commoner was included, for, as we noted earlier Rama VI's policy had been to encourage commoners to share in the responsibility of government. In 1929 Thailand was badly hit by the world economic depression, which seriously affected the price of the country's chief export, rice. Again expenditure greatly exceeded revenue, and further retrenchment was necessary. It was the reduction in the salaries and the numbers of government officials which brought about the crisis of 1932. Beginning with a conspiracy of army and navy officials and civil servants, which the Minister of the Interior failed to deal with effectively, it ended in the revolution of 24 June 1932 and the change of Thailand's regime from absolute monarchy to constitutional democratic government with a constitutional monarch (99: 170–2).

The effect of this on the status of the Buddhist Sangha might have been more drastic than it was, considering the sensitive relationship which existed between the royal house and the Sangha. In Burma the overthrow of the kings had adverse consequences for state Buddhism. But the absolute monarchy in Burma which was displaced by the British in 1885 differed in a number of important ways from Thai monarchy in the twentieth century. Moreover, the Burmese monarchy was replaced by rulers from an alien culture who had very little, if any, sympathy with the traditions of Burmese Buddhism, while in Thailand in 1932 absolute monarchy was replaced by a constitutional form which allowed for continuity in the same line of succession and in the same cultural and religious tradition.

The revolution of 1932 in Thailand was primarily a constitutional and political matter. It did not affect the traditional values of Thai society. It did not even remove the royal house or end its influence. As William Siffin comments: 'After 1932 the importance of the king lay more in his existence than in his actions' (93: 138).

What was entailed for the Buddhist Sangha, as for the country's political system, was a gradual change beneath the surface. Nanavara, Vajiranana's quietly capable successor as patriarch, undoubtedly played an influential part in steadying the situation between the Sangha and the government immediately after the coup, and provided an excellent example of the adaptability of the Thai Sangha, which, an observer in Thailand has noted, 'is at once the secret of its revival and an integral part of its creed' (107:641). Reform of the Sangha and adaptation to meet contemporary needs was already in progress before 1932, under the Patriarch Vajiranana, and before that it had been going on since Mongkut's time at least.

Under Thailand's new constitution after 1932 discussions concerning the Buddhist Sangha took place in the legislative Assembly, and occasionally some harsh notes of criticism of the monks were heard. In 1934, for example, when a proposal for the building of 122 new wats was being debated, one member of the Assembly voiced the opinion that the monks were lazy and socially useless, but this idea met with general disapproval from the rest of the Assembly. Even when another proposal, to employ monks as teachers under the government education scheme, was made, only a few members opposed the idea, on the ground that the monks were incompetent; the majority of the Assembly rejected this view. In fact the monks co-operated very readily when, in 1934, a course in teacher training was established for them (107:639f).

Buddhism ceased to be the state religion in Thailand in 1932, in the sense that it was not compulsory for anyone to follow Buddhist belief and practice. There was one exception to this, namely the king, who according to the new constitution was required to be a Buddhist: 'The King shall profess the Buddhist faith and is the upholder of religion.' Everyone else was 'entirely free to profess any religion or creed and to exercise the form of worship in accordance with his own belief, provided that it is not contrary to the duties of a national, or to public order, or to public morals' (49:208). On the whole the result of this was to popularise Buddhism; in the years between 1942 and 1963 the Sangha was given a constitutional form of government similar to that of the temporal government. This was a step for which the Patriarch Vajiranana's reforms in the organisation of the Sangha had already prepared the way.

The number of monasteries showed a slight increase between

1932 and 1937, from about 17,100 to about 17,400. There was said to be one monastery to every 800 people in central Thailand at this period. In the south of Thailand the ratio was one to every 863, in the east one to 500, and in the north one to every 446 (107:629). The slight increase in the number of monasteries occurred in spite of the policy of the new constitutional government, which aimed at encouraging people to repair old wats and to gain merit in other ways, such as the building of schools and hospitals. But this latter was also the continuation of a policy which had already been advocated by King Mongkut about eighty years earlier.

Buddhist education in Thailand developed considerably in the 1930s. The rank of Nak Dhamma or 'Dhamma Scholar' which the Patriarch Vijaranana had introduced in 1910, for monks intending to remain only a few months and who took a short course of Dhamma studies, using only Thai language, was extended in 1929 to include laymen also. The only difference in the syllabus was the omission, in the case of laymen, of the Vinaya rules. The laymen's course was known as Dhamma-suksa, or 'Dhamma education'. For monks intending to remain longer in the monastic life there were the higher grades of Buddhist education based on the use of Pali language. The numbers of the students in these various courses during the period between 1926/27 and 1936/37 is as follows (49:209 and 121:15):

	Dhamma Scholars	Pali Scholars	Pali Scholars as % of total
1926/27	16,454	4,700	22·21
1929/30	38,434	7,846	16·95
1933/34	55,547	8,954	13·88
1936/37	69,357	9,551	12·10

The number of monks in Thailand increased proportionately to the general population during the 1930s. The number of monks undertaking Pali studies in the decade from 1927 to 1937 more than doubled (4,700 to 9,551). As for the number of Dhamma scholars (using only Thai), it will be seen that in 1937 this was more than four times what it had been in 1927. Thus the extent of Pali scholarship relative to the total scholarship declined during these years. It was in the period after 1932 that lay Buddhists began to take part in public discussion of religious affairs in a way which in former days would have been considered improper

(49:217). The layman's part as a religious teacher also increased. Writing at the end of the 1930s Landon reports:

Religious books are included as part of the regular curriculum in all schools, non-Buddhist as well as Buddhist. They are taught, for the most part, by teachers who are laymen. Regular times are set aside for devotional exercises in which pupils and teachers take part. Many, probably most, schools have images of the Buddha which are used in these exercises. The pupils sometimes bring flowers and do obeisance before the images. Monks are invited to preach at such services. Thus, although the monk is less prominent in the educational field, religious and secular, religious teaching of children is widespread (49:219).

As in Sri Lanka and Burma, there was a growth, though here rather slighter, of what was called the Young Buddhists' Association, from about 1931. The intention of the movement in Thailand (which began at Korat) was of a general educational kind primarily, but it had the effect of stimulating interest in the study of Buddhism among lay people. One of the great needs which was felt in this period was for a Thai version of the Pali Buddhist canonical scriptures, the Tipitaka. This was allied to another need which began to be expressed, namely for the use of Thai language in public devotions, so that there might be better understanding of the meaning of what was done.

The general increase in lay participation in Buddhist affairs meant also the beginning of a more critical attitude towards the place held in Thai religion by the spirit cults, and by practices of Brahmanical origin. More emphasis began to be placed on the ethical and moral aspects of Thai Buddhism. One of the text books widely used in the schools, written by Princess Phun, suggests that all homes should have an image of the Buddha, and that the Buddha should be reverenced, not as a god, but as a wise teacher and as an exemplar in the matter of conduct: one should think more of others than of oneself and should realise the importance of moral character and good works. It has been observed that the book has nothing to say about the traditional Buddhist heavens and hells or about nirvana, the emphasis being rather on the idea that the reward of a good life is happiness in this world (49:221f). A similar example of a slight redirection of emphasis is found in an address given by the Prime Minister to students in 1937 (49:230f). The object of the Dhamma, he said, was to eradicate evils and encourage the cultivation of virtues. The evils which were to be eradicated were, he said, greediness, revengefulness, pride, haughtiness, snobbishness, miserliness, stubbornness, jealousy, resentfulness, dishonesty, arrogance, anger, boastfulness, intemperance, selfishness and undue self-assertiveness. The virtues which were to be cultivated were intelligent generosity, thoughtfulness, uprightness, endurance and contentment, honesty, humility, gratefulness, graciousness and sincerity. The lists are not traditionally Buddhist, but on the other hand they are consonant with traditional values. What was being offered was a restatement of *Thai* Buddhist morality.

Pride, haughtiness and arrogance, however, do not seem to have been successfully eliminated from Thai consciousness, as the policy under the military dictator, Pibul Songgram, shows. Pibul came to power in 1938 and a prominent feature of his rule was 'the wave of chauvinistic nationalism which swept the country' (108:159). This showed itself in a new arrogance towards the Muslims who formed about 85 per cent of the population of the four southern provinces of Patani, Satul, Yala and Naradhivas. These provinces are linguistically and culturally part of Muslim Malaya, but were annexed by Thailand in 1832. The chauvinism of Pibul's Thailand showed itself particularly towards non-Thai minorities, Chinese and Malay. The Muslims of the southern provinces came under increasing pressure. 'Efforts to Siamize them included compelling them to adopt Thai dress, language and customs, and in 1941 their exemption from the enforcement of Buddhist law relating to marriage and inheritance was withdrawn despite their strong objections' (108:159).

Burma's Marxists

It was from nationalism, rather than from Buddhism, that Burma's early Marxism grew (106). It was among the most intensely nationalistic of the younger generation in the 1930s that Marxist ideology began to provide an additional dimension to their view of the situation. They began to be conversant with Marxist ideas, and saw British rule in Burma as imperialist exploitation arising out of the nature and the necessities of capitalism. Copies of *Capital* in English and some of the writings of Lenin came into the hands of students in Rangoon who were active in the nationalist movement after 1931 (110:297). But such Marxist anti-colonialism had the effect of bringing Buddhism into the political arena too. As elsewhere in Asia, the contrast between the industrial and commercial expansion of Britain, sanctioned and possibly encouraged by the Protestant ethic on the one hand and what was now seen as the generally socialistic emphasis of Buddhism on the other, began to be pointed out. Thus: 'The spirit of Buddhism is essentially socialistic, that is to say it teaches concerted action [samanartha] for social ends. It is therefore totally opposed to that industrialism which, with merciless struggle for wealth as the one supreme object of human effort, is eating the very vitals of the so-called advanced nations of the world' (69:45). Similar polemics were directed against the economic and special injustices associated with Protestantism; this was done from the point of view of the upholders of the Buddhist 'Middle Way' (in this case, between luxury and poverty) in the Journal of the Maha Bodhi Society (42, 10–12, 1919:127). On the other hand, there were Buddhist writers in Burma in the 1930s who rejected any idea of affinity between Buddhism and Marxism. These included both monks and laymen. Some saw Marxism as positively anti-Buddhist. They argued that communism seeks to destroy religion; that Buddhism is ill-attuned to the 'herd-mentality' of communism; and that the view of the world and of the life of man which is contained in Marxist doctrine is incompatible with the teaching of the Buddha and contrary to the law of Karma (*New Burma*, 20 July 1938). On the whole, however, what were understood as the ideas of Marxism were accepted, so strong was the resentment of imperialist rule among the emerging nationalist leaders.

Constitutional changes in Thai government and Buddhism

In Thailand the consequences of the centralisation and standardisation of religion have developed steadily throughout the years of the twentieth century so far. The second stage was marked by the Sangha Administration Act of 1941. This was the expression and outcome of the events of the 1930s. The thirties in Thailand were a period of political upheaval. In the years following the coup of 1932 organised by defence services officers, the major immediate effect of which was to change the status of the king from an absolute to a constitutional monarch, there were attempts to establish democracy, both as a system of political government and even in the government of the Sangha. But in both cases these attempts were overcome by the more authoritarian element, represented mainly by the Thai army. By 1941 this element was moving towards the full consolidation of its power, but still needing to tread warily and give the impression of some deference to democracy. The Sangha Administration Act of 1941 was the instrument whereby this was done, and a potentially rebellious movement in the Sangha was headed off. For the constitutional revolution of 1932 had generated a mild epidemic of democratic fever, both in politics and in the Sangha. There were monks who were suggesting that just as absolute monarchy had given place to a constitutional form of responsible government so too should the absolute authority of abbots of monasteries, which the 1902 Sangha Act had established, now give way to more democratic methods of administering the life of monasteries. The 1941 Sangha Act did make some concessions to the spirit of democracy. An ecclesiastical assembly was set up, consisting of forty-five members appointed by the supreme patriarch. The ecclesiastical 'cabinet' or executive body was made responsible to the ecclesiastical assembly and the patriarch's personal power of executive action was limited (20:37). There were one or two other significant changes. The minister of religious affairs, provided for in 1902, whose function it was to mediate between the Sangha and the government, was superseded by the Minister of Education, whose responsibility this now became. As Tambiah comments, this is indicative of the shift the Thai government was making towards tighter lay political control of the Buddhist Sangha (102:251).

Buddhist Burma under Japanese rule

The mood of many of the Burmese people and certainly of the Burmese national leaders by 1941, when Japan entered the war against the Western powers, was one of readiness to welcome the occupation of Burma by the Japanese as fellow Asians and fellow Buddhists. In the words of Prime Minister Ba Maw they felt 'a new conviction that their country would be great again and Buddhism recover its old glory' (4:175). The kind of greatness which was meant, according to Ba Maw, was that of the days when (under Bodawpaya) 'Burmese armies had marched into Thailand in the East, and Assam and Manipur in the north west, and Yunnan in the north East', for they were (in the first days of the Japanese conquest) already marching alongside the army of the divine emperor. But Burmese hopes were soon disappointed. What followed was 'a reign of terror' (4:176). 'It is true that the war itself and the conditions it created were brutal and brutalising, but these militarists surpassed all others the Burmese had ever known. The brutality, arrogance, and racial pretensions of these men remained among the deepest Burmese memories of the war years' (4:180). Another Burmese writer, not given to underestimating the damage done by the British rule in Burma, records his memories as follows: 'The period of Japanese military rule lasted only three years, but to the Burmese people it was more irksome than some sixty years of British rule . . . The Japanese imposed a reign of terror' (37:301). These were the realities of coexistence with 'fellow Buddhists' of another nationality.

Ba Maw had at first hoped for much from co-operation with the Japanese; he himself was not disappointed. He was made 'Adipadi', or national leader, by the occupying power under a new arrangement of the affairs of the Burman state which was 'essentially fascist and Japanese in character' (13:456). He selected Bandoola U Sein to help popularise the 'Trust Japan' programme; Bandoola U Sein's title was Minister of Religious Development and Propaganda, itself an indication of the role Ba Maw intended Buddhism to play. Not himself a Buddhist by up-bringing (he was born in a Christian family with some Armenian connections and was educated in law at Cambridge and Bordeaux), his attitude to the Buddhist Sangha can best be described as opportunist. He had made caustic reference to 'Burma's 250,000 idle *pongyis*' (114:116), but later he found it convenient to ac-knowledge the Sangha's influence, and publicly stated that monks 'make very good propagandists as all of us know'. One of his first efforts to enlist monks in his propaganda machine was the setting up of the Dobama Synyetha Asiayone, or Burmese People's Monks' Association, on the basis that: all monks must (1) collaborate in the construction of New Burma; (2) purge Burma of all enemies of Nippon and Burma; (3) foster friendly Nippon-Burma relations; and (4) carry out a positive religious programme of benefit to the Burmese people (114:151). As Adipadi (leader) of Burma, Ba Maw made his confession of faith in the Buddha, the Dhamma, and the Sangha and pledged himself to 'defend the Buddhist faith like the royal defenders of old'. He engaged in various public displays of his new Buddhist piety. Had he been sincere in his sentiments no doubt Burmese Buddhists would have welcomed his change of heart, but to those closest to him he appeared simply to be toadying to political monks. U Nu in his account of Burma during the Japanese occupation lavished much praise on Ba Maw, but with regard to the cynical use Ba Maw made of the Buddhist Sangha he had this to say: 'I firmly believe that men who lean on *pongyis* in politics are mere opportunists. The men who drag *pongyis* into politics should be pitied because they do not know how sinfully they are acting . . . Although the *pongyi* can escape penalty by doing penance, this does not relieve the guilt incurred by the man who has made use of him' (13: 464f).

Ba Maw's association with Bandoola U Sein only increases doubt about his religious consistency. It is said that Ba Maw had to try hard to swallow the kind of astrological warnings which Bandoola U Sein kept coming up with, although we are also told that Ba Maw consulted a palmist in 1943 in order to know whether he would be assassinated (13: 463). Later, when the war had begun to take a bad turn for Japan and thus for Ba Maw, he asked the Burmese people to make special offerings and prayers to the Nats, the guardian spirits.

So far as the Buddhist Sangha was concerned, the result of Ba Maw's attempts to use monks for propaganda purposes was at first to harden the divisions within the Sangha between those who were politically active as nationalists and those who were not. The divisions had been there throughout the 1930s; the president of the YMBA of Rangoon at a meeting in 1939 had referred to the danger to the life of the Sangha of becoming actively involved in political struggle: 'participation in politics is the main cause of splits' (114:152).

But as the Japanese occupation continued it became clear that the smooth official utterances of Japanese spokesmen, intended to encourage Buddhist monks in Burma to support the Japanese 'Great East Asia Co-Prosperity Sphere', were not matched by the actions and attitudes of the Japanese army. Monks suffered forcible indignities at the hands of the soldiers, monasteries were used for the stabling of horses, shrines were desecrated and pagoda treasures were stolen. Such behaviour was utterly offensive to most of Burma's Buddhists, lay and ordained, and the result was in the end that many of the monks refused to be involved any longer in the affairs of Ba Maw and the Japanese, and so 'the wartime experiences of the Sangha . . . eliminated the pongyis as an organised political power on the national level' (114:152).

What emerges from Burma's history during this period, from 1900 to the end of the Second World War, is that there was a marked and growing polarisation of the Sangha during the middle part of the period, a polarisation between the traditional village monk whose principal concerns were those of the monastery and village life and the political monks whose principal concerns were those of nationhood. This occurred mainly during the middle years of the period and reached its climax in the thirties, when for a while more and more monks, even in the villages, were drawn into participation in political or quasi-political issues. Then, in the forties, when the Sangha was at first blatantly exploited and later treated with contempt by Burma's Japanese rulers, a reaction set in as monks everywhere became disenchanted with the political realm and alienated from affairs of the state. How permanent this disenchantment and alienation were we shall now have to consider in connection with the history of the post-war period, from 1945 to the present day.

5

Buddhism and Nationalism in the Post-War World

The dilemma : tradition versus modernity

The three decades after the end of the Second World War were a time of great outward change in South–East Asia, as elsewhere. When the tide of Japanese occupation had receded in 1945 the question naturally arose: who should rule now? Some attempts were made in the former European colonies – Burma, Laos and Cambodia – to reimpose European rule, but these were short-lived. In Thailand an experiment was made with democratic government and that also was short-lived; thereafter, under a façade of monarchy, the country was governed by an army elite backed for most of this period by the United States. In all Buddhist countries of South–East Asia the influence of a new ideology, communism, had now to be taken into serious account, whether it was an active force or only potential. This became more marked after 1949 when, along the northern border of South–East Asia, the People's Republic of China came into existence. The shape of events in the succeeding decades was already beginning to be discernible by 1956, when the Buddhists of Asia gathered to usher in the second half of five thousand years of Buddhism. Although it is traditionally believed (by the orthodox) that Buddhism must decline during this forthcoming period and finally disappear, after which Maitreya, the next Buddha, will appear, nevertheless, the approach of the 2,500th anniversary was accompanied by a sense of expectancy, almost of a messianic kind, in the countries of South–East Asia. It was believed popularly that 'a great renovation of Religion and a great expansion of its

Law shall come 2,500 years after the Parinirvana of the Buddha', and that 'there shall, when Buddhism will have completed 2,500 years, be established a Buddhist state in Ceylon' (86: 206). This was one of the causes leading to the demand for a Buddhist state in Ceylon; but the idea and the demand were not confined to that island. In Burma also there was a great popular feeling that the country should now once again become a Buddhist kingdom, as it had been only a little more than sixty years before, when a Burmese Buddhist king had reigned in Mandalay. But this was not to be; other forces, secular and Marxist, were present now, and Burma's national leaders were not unanimously in favour of what to many of them the establishment of a Buddhist kingdom would be, simply a return to the past.

A noticeable feature of the period was the growth of the practice of meditation among lay people, and of special provision for learning the methods of meditation. 'In recent times its revival received an impetus first in Burma and then in other countries. The meditation centres of Burma attracted people from all parts of the world' (42, April 1972: 74). One among a number of meditation centres was that established in Rangoon by U Ba Khin in 1952. This was used mainly by lay Buddhists, mostly of the professional classes, both Burmese and Western, and has become one of the better known of such centres. This was another kind of effect produced by the increasingly secular quality of urban life in Burma and elsewhere. This lay participation in an activity which is traditionally associated with the monastery is a characteristic feature of Buddhism in modern societies.

In Thailand an old tradition received a new emphasis during the post-war years, that of the forest hermitage. There are in the north-east a number of 'monasteries' which consist mainly of huts or cottages scattered about in the forest, intended primarily for monks and laymen who wish to specialise in meditation. A similar, very well-known forest meditation centre in the south of Thailand is Wat Suan Moke, two and a half miles from the town of Chaiya. There are altogether about twenty of the better known meditation centres of this kind in Thailand.

Another development of the immediate post-war years was the World Fellowship of Buddhists. The initiative for this came from the All-Ceylon Buddhist Congress which, at its twenty-eighth annual session in December 1947, passed a resolution that plans should be made to invite representatives from various Buddhist countries to a conference 'for the purpose of bringing closer together the Buddhists of the world'. In June 1950 the World Fellowship of Buddhists came into existence, with headquarters first in Colombo, then for a short while in Rangoon, and finally in Bangkok. The third general Conference of the Fellowship was held in Rangoon in 1954, and coincided with the beginning of the two-year period of preparation for the 2,500th anniversary celebrations which the Prime Minister of Burma, U Nu, and the Burmese government arranged in Rangoon in 1956. While this was in some respects an international Buddhist occasion – the Sixth Buddhist Council – it served a national purpose also; at a time when Burma, newly independent of British rule, was going through severe internal troubles, political and ethnic, the Buddhist Council served to focus attention on the great traditions and past splendours of the Buddhist world, of which Burma rightly felt herself a major part.

The disturbances within Burma were the inevitable result of the convergence of various currents, economic, political and ideological. While most of the ordinary people had remained unchanged in their simple devotion to Buddhism, there were some, and among the monks it was a higher percentage, who were not content to return to the traditionalism of the past. Monks had learnt to be politically active in the national cause, under colonial rule, and it seemed to many of them in the late forties and fifties that political action was still demanded of them, in a period of insurgency of communists and minority peoples such as the Karens. Once monks had learnt to take a hand in public affairs, and there were many who had, it was difficult for them to give up.

Even if the Buddhists of South–East Asia had wished to return to the traditional society they had once known it would have been as difficult for them as it is for any other group of people in the modern world. Burma's leaders, Buddhist though they were, *chose*, in 1948, to make their newly independent nation not a Buddhist kingdom as before but a secular modern republic. This is but one indication of the fact that Burma and the neighbouring Buddhist countries of South–East Asia were being drawn headlong into the stream of world trends and events. In spite of themselves they have continued to be dragged along in that stream during the decades since. However, in the early 1950s this view of Burma's future as a secular, developing country was beginning to be challenged, and was thereafter modified by the very pious Buddhist Prime Minister U Nu. In addition to devoting considerable resources to the setting up of the Sixth

Buddhist Council in Rangoon in 1956, he formed the ambition of making Burma once again a constitutionally Buddhist state. In the face of much opposition from minority groups the constitutional change was put into effect in 1961; a fuller account of this will be given later.

The professional bearers of Buddhism, the bhikkhus, were divided among themselves over the issues of tradition and modernisation. Some, who were vociferous at this time, wanted to see the Buddhist polity of the pre-British period restored; but this seemed to others to entail a return to traditional roles and attitudes for monks, and not all wished to accept the old roles. Modern ways of thought had made an indelible mark on the minds of some sections of the Sangha at least, and modern social and political policies and programmes had a strong attraction for those who were aware, however dimly, of the tremendous tasks of nation building. But the old ways, too, had an appeal, for much of the modern world looked hideous from the quietness and seclusion of a Burmese Buddhist monastery.

Popular Burmese Buddhist values

Burmese Buddhism, with its characteristically rural ambience and its limited economic aims, in general presents a strong contrast to many of the presuppositions, norms, and values of the industrialised and possibly overdeveloped world of the West. Certainly from the point of view of the latter, 'the impact of Buddhist cultural values upon questions of economic change' is seen in terms of 'cultural resistance'. Such is the judgement made by a Westernised Burman, Mya Maung, now teaching in the United States (68:533). This is an example of the tendency which has been observed among some economists, when faced with the need to explain lack of economic growth, and when pure economic analysis alone appears inadequate, to look around for a culprit among the non-economic or background factors and, very often, to settle on cultural values as being chiefly to blame.

In Burma's case, however, there are two other 'background' factors which are vastly more important, namely Burma's experience of colonial rule and the effect on Burma of the Second World War, which was more severe and chronic than in any other country in South–East Asia.

Throughout most of Burma's history her peoples enjoyed a reasonable level of subsistence; the delta and valley lowland

region is extremely fertile and population density has been low by
any standards. But the people of Burma were not enjoying a
reasonable level of subsistence by the time British colonial rule
was drawing to a close in the 1930s. The economic condition of
the Burmese people during those last years was described by
J. S. Furnivall, a British civil servant of many years service in
Burma, in his book *Colonial Policy and Practice*. He gives a
detailed analysis of the effects of the British *laissez-faire* policy
in respect of the economic development of Burma and demonstrates its effect upon the Burmese people in terms of rural in-
debtedness and agrarian distress and, along with this, 'the multi-
plication of litigation and crime'. Economic freedom under
British rule, says Furnivall, 'merely allowed the people to pile
up debt and lose their land (i.e. to Indian moneylenders)'
(24:216). Walinsky endorses this in his *Economic Development
in Burma, 1951–60*. In dealing with the background to the situation
inherited by the Burmese in 1947 he devotes a section to out-
lining the economic situation in the late 1930s, so far as the
Burmese farmer was concerned. 'While other prices rose [on the
world markets] the price of rice dropped sharply. [Indian] moneylenders called in their loans. The pace of foreclosure quickened
and economic distress in the countryside did much to stimulate
the growth of political unrest, and, eventually, race riots between
the Burmese and Indians in Rangoon' (117:24). An analysis of
Burma's economic condition by a group of Japanese economists,
published in Tokyo in 1961, was highly critical of the 'typical
mono-culture economic structure wherein approximately 70 per
cent of the gross exports are dependent on rice exports' (2:148).
This group of economists, like Furnivall and Walinsky, point to
the reason for this, in British policy. The delta region of lower
Burma was sparsely populated at the beginning of British rule.
Burma, it must be remembered, was administered as a province of
British India. India had a surplus of labour and some 'richly
adventurous usuristic capital' (2:252), whereas Burma had no
surplus of either. British policy allowed Indian labour and
capital to flow into lower Burma and develop the whole area
as a rice-bowl; 'not only did the Indian Chettyars move in as
farming-village usurers in response to the capital requirements of
farmers in the newly opened lands, but the British assisted the
immigration of Indians and Indian labour emigration through
subsidies and legal provisions' (2:252). The result of this excessive
development of rice for export left Burma's economy highly

vulnerable; Burma was, moreover, 'placed in an inferior position not only with respect to commercial and industrial financing but even in the area of labour' (2:253). Apart from this, British control of Burma was in the interests of extractive industries such as teak and oil, which meant only the simple processing of these materials for export and sale by British-owned companies. The economy was a typically colonial one, as little diversified industrially as it was agriculturally.

To this situation of economic imbalance and rural distress were then added the physical, social and political effects of the Second World War, in which Burma was a major theatre of war. Lucian Pye, in his study of Burma's efforts to build up her nationhood again from 1947, takes a curiously perfunctory view of the damage which the war between Japan and the West did to Burma. He considers that in view of Burma's mineral resources, her plentiful food supplies (rice), and the river Irrawaddy providing 'a natural and economical means of transportation' it is difficult to understand why Burma's economy did not develop more rapidly than it had done (by the time he was writing, just before 1962). 'The fact that there are so few [*sic*] objective handicaps to economic development in Burma suggests the extreme importance of non-objective considerations . . . The fact that Burmese production, fifteen years after World War II, has just been restored to pre-war levels suggests that the obstacles to its development may fall largely in the realm of political relations, psychological attitudes, and cultural values' (82:60). To ignore the effects of colonialism and war on independent Burma's economy make it possible for him to give major prominence to 'psychological attitudes and cultural values'. He mentions, only to dismiss summarily, the fact that Burma was a major scene of the fighting in the Second World War.

This is not the view of the Japanese economists who were making their survey of Burma's economic situation at about the time that Pye was writing. Their report emphasises that outside of Japan itself, which suffered atomic bombing by the U.S.A., 'war damage in Burma was the greatest of any nation in Asia' (2:183). The effect on agricultural production was disastrous, for a variety of reasons. Livestock needed for ploughing suffered a large decrease in numbers owing to requisitioning by the Japanese army and disease. A legacy of the disturbed conditions of a country under occupation was the poor state of law and order, and this in turn hampered 'the orderly economic activity of the farming villages', for reasons concerned with the farmers' routine, which the report analyses in detail (2:223). The farmer's 'will to produce' had been seriously affected by all this. Above all, two major campaigns were fought across the whole extent of the country, in 1942 when the British retreated into India before the invading Japanese, and then in 1945 when the 'Allies bombed and fought their way back' across the country. In the course of the latter campaign, and the destruction wrought by both the retreating Japanese and the advancing Allies, Burma lost what capital facilities she had, such as transport, telecommunications, and electric power supply plants. 'Even her farmlands were left devastated' (2:254). Burma Railways had practically ceased operating, since 80 per cent of its property had been destroyed.

It took until the end of the 1950s to repair the physical damage in the countryside, but not all the fertile paddy land which had reverted to jungle had been reoccupied and cultivated again by then, owing to depopulation of some areas. Hence, it is not surprising that in the preface to his *Colonial Policy and Practice* Furnivall wrote: 'It is a tumbled house which they inherit . . . exports have fallen by two-thirds of the pre-war figure of £37 million. The annual revenue covers only a third of the current expenditure, and the national debt of £110 million (about seven times the revenue) is rapidly increasing . . . In a troubled world, though less acquainted with affairs than their old rulers, they face a situation far more difficult' (24:xi). 'Less acquainted with affairs' may be taken as a reference to the fact that under British rule the Burmese had practically no experience of public administration. The Indian Civil Service was virtually closed to them (except the 'Class II Burma Civil Service', to which was entrusted only the most routine of administrative tasks).

Independent Burma's post-war government was faced with very great internal political strife also. Even had they had the experience of administration, and even *had* they a viable economy to administer, it would still have been an extremely difficult task, in view of the political division, inter-regional conflicts, and communist insurgency they had to deal with.

If, therefore, Burma's development in the years following 1947 was slower than that of some other countries there are many reasons for it, economic and non-economic. And among the non-economic reasons it is not necessary to look immediately at Burmese Buddhist culture. The cultural factor was not the major obstacle to economic development by any means. The primary problem was the inherited economic structure, 'the excessive reliance on rice production and exports which results in the entire financing structure being highly unstable . . .' and, as we have seen, 'the fundamental responsibility for this situation should be placed on the British colonial system which forced this monocultural system on Burma' (2:605). If, as some have tried to argue, cultural resistance to economic change was to blame, something like this cultural resistance would have operated also in neighbouring Thailand, whose culture is a compound of similar elements to that of Burma. The main difference is that Thailand escaped European colonisation. Thailand's economic development since the Second World War seems to have been one of comfortable moderation between the poverty of post-colonial Burma and the booming entrepreneurial prosperity of Japan. The significant differences between the two cases, Burma and Thailand, lie somewhere other than in the sphere of cultural values.

Burmese Buddhist values and capitalism

There is, however, the other equally significant difference just noted; namely between Thailand and Japan. This leads us to another aspect of the relation between Burmese Buddhist culture and economic development, an aspect of Buddhism which was observed by Max Weber, that its values do not find natural expression in a capitalist economy. We return, therefore, to the examination of Mya Maung's thesis, that Buddhism has been largely responsible for slow economic development in Burma, because of its resistance to economic change.

In pursuit of this thesis attention is drawn to the 'lack of effort to improve one's economic position' said to be found in Burmese society (68:528). This is attributed by Mya Maung to widespread adherence to the 'Buddhist doctrine' of karma. This doctrine, it is said, emphasises the uselessness of effort, since a man receives in this life only those boons to which his previous karma has entitled him. Since he believes his own effort will avail nothing he has no incentive to make any effort, and this lack of incentive will clearly have an inhibiting effect on economic progress. Such is the theory according to Mya Maung; what it ignores is the fact that Buddhist doctrine does *not* discourage moral effort. It is remarkable that anyone claiming to expound Buddhist doctrine and values should miss so elementary a point.

Another way in which, according to this theory, Buddhist

attitudes discourage economic progress is through the general view of life presented by Buddhism, as something characterised by suffering and impermanence. This, says Mya Maung, suggests to the Burman 'the futility of the desire for goods, wealth, position and power' (68:528). This, however, is a considerable oversimplification.

Buddhist cultural values might appear to the observer who has an eye to the development of capital resources to affect economic development adversely by reason of the 'big spending' indulged in by the Burmese Buddhist in the interests of merit-acquiring through dana. Such merit-making expenditure is usually devoted to lavish hospitality and entertainment for friends and neighbours, and to ceremonial banquets for members of the Sangha. Spiro provides a detailed account of expenditure on merit-making activities (97:456ff). The major forms of expenditure are those connected with the Sangha. These are: (1) the *initiation ceremony* : the expenses for this are paid by the family whose son is being initiated into the Sangha, and the amount spent can vary from 200 to 5,000 kyats (the average annual income in rural central Burma where Spiro's data come from is about 1,000 kyats); (2) *collective offering of robes* to members of the Sangha; this is done in one month of the year, the robe-offering season, but a single family may be involved in five or six such offerings. The most expensive of these robe-offering ceremonies known to Spiro cost 10,000 kyats; (3) *funerals of members of the Sangha* in a small, thirty-family village can cost about 2,000 kyats (97: 457). Each family in such a case contributes from 40 to 75 kyats. Other expenses are special offerings of food to members of the Sangha, the construction and repair of pagodas, and the regular daily feeding of the Sangha. The last item alone takes about 10 per cent of the income of the family, according to Spiro. His conclusion is that 'the typical upper Burmese village is reported to spend from 30 to 40 per cent of its net disposable cash income on dana and relative activities' (97:459). These figures are derived from estimates given to Spiro by village elders in fifteen villages in upper Burma. His own estimate is lower, based on a detailed house to house survey; he reckons it as 25 per cent. It is, he says, 'no exaggeration to say that the economy of rural Burma is geared to the overriding goal of the accumulation of wealth as a means to acquiring merit' (97:459).

Thus, in Burma, the pursuit of traditional religious and social values, says Spiro, 'provides a powerful motive for economic action'. However, it is important to note that the money which becomes available at harvest time, when the farmer sells his surplus, is channelled into what are from the entrepreneurial point of view unproductive activities. It is spent in maintaining what the Burmese experience as a pleasurable existence now, in this life, and in ensuring improved chances of an even more pleasurable existence next time. Max Weber, while he was wrong in his analysis of Buddhism at some points, was probably right when he said of Buddhism in this case that 'there evolved no "capitalist spirit" in the sense that is distinctive of ascetic Protestantism' (120:269). Unlike Weber's Puritan, 'the Burmese Buddhist views worldly pleasures as a boon to be enjoyed'. The money which the Burmese farmer receives in payment for his produce is not usually available even as spare cash long enough to be used for short-term investment, as for example the savings of the Malay Muslim towards his journey to Mecca are. In Burma, the season of festivity follows close upon the harvest and surplus cash is soon spent. Hence there can be little disagreement with Spiro's conclusion that 'it can hardly be doubted that over a period of successive generations, the channeling of Burmese savings into economic investments rather than religion would have made a significant difference in the development and growth of the Burmese economy' (97:463). This may well be true; but it is doubtful whether the Burmese economy which might have resulted if the money had been so channelled would have been preferable to the majority of Burmese Buddhists.

Burmese Buddhist values and the environment

Even if Burmese Buddhists were all alerted to the situation and were made to realise that there were alternative ways of using their surplus earnings, it is by no means likely that they would choose to avail themselves of them, in the sense of engaging in competitive entrepreneurial activity. E. F. Schumacher, who served the Government of Burma as economic adviser from 1955 to 1962, has pointed out that Burmese Buddhists have their own view of what is the ultimate economic goal (90:695ff). The Burmese are not obliged to accept the presupposition of the Westerner that industrialisation is good because it brings increased consumption of material goods, and thus a so-called higher standard of living. Burmese culture is geared to a more modest economic goal than that of the Western one of total exploitation of every possible material substance which man can lay his hands on. It is geared to low consumption rather than high, especially of such goods as fuel, cloth, housing material and even, to some extent, food. The less that is consumed annually the better. The aim is 'to obtain the maximum of well being with the minimum of consumption', Schumacher observes (90:698). 'Thus, if the purpose of clothing is a certain amount of temperature, comfort and an attractive appearance, the task is to attain this purpose with the smallest annual destruction of cloth and with the help of designs that involve the smallest possible input of toil. The less toil there is, the more time and strength is left for artistic creativity. It would be highly uneconomic, for instance, to go in for complicated tailoring, like the modern West, when a much more beautiful effect can be achieved by the skilful draping of uncut material. It would be the height of folly to make the material so that it should wear out quickly and the height of barbarity to make anything ugly, shabby or mean. What has just been said about clothing applies equally to all human requirements' (90:698).

Added to his emphasis on simplicity in everyday living standards is the Buddhist emphasis on non-violence. These two emphases have been central to the recognised life-style of the Buddhist layman since the time of Asoka. 'It is good not to kill living beings' is the message to the citizens of his realm which occurs in the Asokan *Rock Edicts* and *Pillar Edicts*. Added to this is the other injunction, to be personally generous, in the whole range of social relationships, which are carefully enumerated, and to adopt a simple style of life: 'It is good not only to spend little, but (also) to own the minimum of property'. Non-violence to all beings is taken to include the physical environment, and certainly the care of trees and avoidance of unnecessary burning of forests (105:264). The present writer recalls a modern example of this which he saw in the gardens of a Thai wat; some new trees had been planted, and were not yet established, so beside them there was a notice in Thai which said, literally, 'please do not hurt the trees'. To use any material resources heedlessly or wastefully would be morally wrong, comments Schumacher. Renewable goods like wood and waterpower should be used with care; non-renewable goods shall be used 'only if they are indispensable, and then only with the greatest care and the most meticulous concern for conservation. To use them heedlessly or extravagantly is an act of violence . . .' (90:699). It may be surmised that Schumacher's presentation of the Theravada Buddhist attitudes on economic affairs is based not so much on the evidence of the Pali canon, although a good case along these lines could be constructed from that source, as on the attitudes of his Buddhist informants in Burma. More than one Westerner has been aware of the different kinds of response which are evoked respectively by the civilisations of India and of Burma. India was seen by the nineteenth-century Englishman in terms of the white man's burden, of the great tasks of reform and enlightenment which needed to be carried out, and of the superiority of his own civilisation. Burma was by contrast a pleasant land with a generally humane society. As one Englishman wrote towards the end of the nineteenth century, 'Coming from half-starved, over-driven India, it is a revelation to see the animals in Burma. The village ponies and cattle and dogs in India are enough to make the heart bleed for their sordid misery, but in Burma they are a delight to the eye . . . The Burman is full of the greatest sympathy towards animals . . . he has no contempt for them; but the gentle toleration of a father to very little children who are stupid and troublesome often, but are very loveable' (28:239). H. Fielding Hall, from one of whose works that quotation is taken, wrote a good deal about the country and the people for whom he had so much affection and admiration. The effect of his writings about Burma and the condition of the common people in a Buddhist civilisation was such that the London *Morning Post* reviewer of one of his books, comparing the social condition of the people of England and Burma at that time, found that 'for the great majority of the working classes the superiority of Western civilisation is a doubtful point' (28: 314). It is much the same today, according to Lucian Pye: 'India now suggests to Americans the urgency of five-year plans and the merits of modern industrial development, while Burma continues to evoke a question as to whether modern life is really the ultimate way' (82:177).

The Buddhist values which gradually permeated Burmese society in the course of the centuries produced an economy which has among its notable characteristics that it is, so far as the individual is concerned, non-acquisitive, and so far as the environment and natural resources are concerned notably less violently exploitative and destructive. The history of the modern West, since the rise of Protestantism, has been characterised by a drive to dominate. The natural world is subject to man, and it is man's divinely ordained task to explore its farthest corners and ransack all its resources; to refrain from doing so, to respect it and honour it for what it is *per se*, would be a sin tantamount to pantheism. And those who regard themselves as the elect, the saved, the chosen of God, have seen it as their proper task to dominate and colonise both politically and 'spiritually' the rest of the world.

For the Buddhist the task is not that of domination, but co-operation. Within Burma, in particular, the non-acquisitive, non-violently exploitative attitude, in terms of modern statehood, was for a time given expression in the creation of a society in which it was hoped that the country's natural and human resources would be respected and used for the common good of all.

But these pious hopes were fading fast by the beginning of the sixties. Burmese rural life may have expressed admirably the humane Buddhist values which were part of Burma's Buddhist inheritance. There was also, however, the political legacy from the Buddhist past: the old assumptions and values of royal Buddhism, assumptions and values which if they had begun to seem hopelessly anachronistic by the end of the eighteenth century without a doubt provided a potent formula for disaster for any Burmese government unwise enough to attempt to revive them in the middle of the twentieth. And that, it seems, is what U Nu, Burma's post-war Prime Minister, tried to do in 1961. Before we consider what did in fact happen, it will be useful to recount briefly the dominant trends in Thai Buddhism during the same period.

The Sangha as a tool of the Thai state

After a series of abortive attempts had been made in the post-war decade to establish democratic government, Thailand suffered yet another of its many coups in September 1957 and Field-Marshal Sarit set up a military bureaucracy which was to last, apart from one brief interval, until the present time; Thailand has been governed virtually by the group of men who rose to power in that coup. One of Sarit's major concerns was to establish national integration, that is to say to eliminate all possible causes of social dissension or conflict, and in this connection he found it necessary to deal with internal disagreements within the Buddhist Sangha. As Yoneo Ishii has put it, 'On October 28, 1960, Sarit issued a high-handed statement that the government was ready to intervene in the affairs of the Buddhist Church at its request to settle the dispute. Finally he decided to reform the ecclesiastical organisation and establish a strong leadership in the Church' (38: 869). The result was a new law, entitled the Buddhist Sangha Act of 1962, which rejected outright the principle of democracy in the affairs of the Sangha and established a centralised system of authority, operating with a hierarchical structure headed by the Supreme Patriarch, and a chain of responsibility from the head of the local monastery, up through the Buddhist head at the village level, the district, the province, and the region to the Council of Elders in Bangkok over whom the Supreme Patriarch exerted direct control. The power of the abbots of monasteries was strengthened and the Sangha was given authority to expel any monks who were disobedient to orders issued by their superiors. This, it should be noted, is not the same as expulsion for the two quite specific reasons given in the canonical Vinaya; this entails expulsion for disobeying *civil* laws. The transforming of the Sangha in Thailand into this new, simple but powerful disciplinary organisation can be described without exaggeration as a crucial new phase in the history of Thai Buddhism. The monks were no longer free to challenge secular authority as they had been, long ago in the old pre-Bangkok days; now, if they challenged the laws of Thailand's military ruler they could simply be disrobed and ejected.

This meant of course that the Sangha could be used much more easily by the government in the pursuit of its own political purposes. The first major use of this power came in 1965, when the Dhammaduta programme was inaugurated, under which monks were sent as 'missionaries' from Bangkok to outlying areas of the country to strengthen the local people's attachment to local Buddhist institutions and to Thai Buddhist ideology. In this way, it was expected, these specially trained Buddhist monks would help to combat the influence of alien ideologies from across Thailand's borders, notably from across the north-east border with Laos, and the southern border with Malaysia. The alien ideology from across these two frontiers which was likely to appeal to the long-neglected and economically depressed people of these areas was any kind of left-wing ideology; of whatever kind it was it would be labelled 'communism' by Bangkok and treated accordingly. J. A. N. Mulder very appropriately has described the task of the specially trained missionary monks sent to these areas as 'a kind of moral rearmament mission'.

Somboon Suksamran, a Thai political scientist and former government official in northern Thailand, has also written at length about the Dhammaduta programme in his *Political Buddhism in South–East Asia* (1977), and has come to the conclusion that the state's use of the monks for this purpose was counter-productive on two points: first, it undermined any possible respect the local people might have felt towards the Buddhist Sangha; and, second, it undermined any respect they might have felt for the government, because of their contempt for a government which resorted to such tactics.

Thus, the nature of the interrelationship of Buddhist monks, political ruler and people has changed dramatically since the days when it could be expressed in terms of a reciprocal three-way relationship. The crucial change came with the setting up of a permanent Thai army in the early years of this century. A fourth factor had now been added. From then on the relationship was one of people, Sangha, king *and* army. After 1932, when the army demonstrated its ultimate power and the king became a constitutional monarch with the army's permission, the pattern was virtually reduced to a threefold: (1) nation; (2) religion-and-king; (3) army. The nature of the situation had changed in the direction of encouraging the people, under the rule of the army, to regard themselves as the nation. Mediating between the army and the nation were the Sangha and the king, valuable to the army rulers as symbols of national identity. From 1962 onwards the Sangha has clearly become a tool of the military rulers, but a tool they find it essential to possess, in the same way that they find the king, because of the veneration in which he is held by the people, a valuable symbol of the nation's identity. The old formula for loyalty, 'Religion, King and Country', continues to be used, but it expresses now only one side of the reality that is the Thai State. The nation, recognising its identity as it is expressed in the politically valuable sacred symbols of Sangha and king, can be ruled by the more or less able manipulation of these tools by the Thai army.

The Buddhist Sangha in Thailand can be seen to have been brought to its present position as the instrument of a military government on account of the central position in the affairs of the state towards which it had been moving for many decades, if not longer. Whatever the political colour of a government, a Sangha which has become so fully integrated an element of the state machinery is likely to suffer the same fate elsewhere. This is evident from what has befallen the Sangha in Laos since the victory of the communists there (see appendix).

The Thai Buddhist Sangha has thus, in the course of the twentieth century, acquired a bureaucratic structure and has had forced upon it an increasing measure of control by Thailand's military rulers. This is in strong contrast to the independent 'congregational' character which it still had at the end of the nineteenth century in some parts of Thailand and which it certainly had in Burma, even under British rule, an independence which it exhibited most clearly of course in its original early Indian setting. The profound respect in which the Buddhist monks are held in rural areas is such that it is highly unlikely that any movements of an alternative religious kind would be generated among rural lay people, and with monks strictly controlled by the central authority the likelihood of nonconformist monks emerging is not great, to say the least. Even among the educated urban lay people of Bangkok there seems to be little potential for any expression of religious nonconformity. Herbert Phillips writes of what he calls the 'selective silence' of Thai intellectuals in Bangkok. He cites a number of characteristics of the condition of Buddhist religion in Thailand today about which Thai intellectuals appear to be indifferent: 'the decline in the viability of Buddhist practice, at least as measured by the number of men entering the monkhood, the [decline in] the number of laymen participating in Buddhist sabbath, the increasing difficulty that urban monks experience in obtaining food on their begging rounds, and the like' (80:330). S. J. Tambiah notes the lavish expenditure by middle-class Buddhist citizens of Bangkok on such devotional articles as temple furniture, statues, religious books, incense, and candles, which the pious purchase to give to monks in order to make merit. But the conclusion to be drawn from all this ritual paraphernalia, he declares, is not that Buddhism is a flourishing religio-social activity, vitally alive and well in Bangkok. Buddhism in Bangkok is a religion of the bourgeoisie, who have a tremendous urge to possess and enjoy the material goods and luxuries associated with affluence. So he concludes that 'the more the Thai participate in this expansionary cycle of wished-for betterment of this worldly life, the more meaningful it is for them as Buddhists to engage in greater and greater gift giving to monks and to temples, and thereby accumulate merit, which they believe will feed back directly into and affect the fortunes of their everyday lives . . . they are appreciative of plenty and desire more than what they have now' (102:509f). Critical or radical religious thought or action seems to be at a very low ebb indeed; ritual activity of a purely conformist kind (and the more conformist the better) seems to be the prevailing characteristic of Thai Buddhist religion among the urban educated classes. The extent to which this religiously and intellectually sterile situation can be explained as a consequence of the authoritarian and bureaucratic structure of Buddhist institutions in Thailand is too large a question to attempt to answer here. What can be reiterated with safety is that all this contrasts strikingly with the richness and independence of Buddhist religious thought before it had ever entered into compromise with monarchical rule, perhaps in Asoka's time. It is possible to disagree with S. J. Tambiah when he says that 'early Buddhism was not merely a salvation quest for the virtuosi but also had a developed view of the world process, of kingship as the ordinating principle of the polity cum society, and that the integral yoking of religion and polity, of Sangha and Kingship, was the armature with which we must begin our investigation' (102:515). It is doubtful whether this primal link between Sangha and monarchy existed in the early period. There is too much in the Pali-canonical material that represents the Buddha as having taken a rather ambivalent attitude towards monarchy, and too much that seems to express a preference for a republican confederation as a form of secular government to enable one to feel happy about Tambiah's view of early Buddhism. Certainly, however, developments occurred in Asoka's reign which modified the early attitudes, and provided the precedent and the model for the pattern of partnership between king and Sangha which then found classical expression in Sri Lanka, and which has now been taken a step further in Thailand. But it is difficult to disagree with what Tambiah says concerning the contrast between, on the one hand, the strong tendency which has been seen in Buddhist countries at various times in the modern period notably in Sri Lanka, Burma and Thailand to make Buddhism the official religion of the state and, on the other hand, the resistance with which India has successfully withstood demands to make Hindu religion the privileged state religion (102:521).

In recent years Thailand's military and bureaucratic elite have made cynical use of the symbols of Buddhism. Perhaps the most blatant example was the return in 1976 of the former military dictator, Thanom Kittikachorn, from exile. For three years

Thailand had had a liberal democratic government, established in 1973 mainly by the student and working-class protest movement (in spite of an attempt by the military clique to crush it, using infantry, tanks and artillery in support of the police). This brief period of democracy was increasingly resented and hated by the privileged upper classes of Bangkok and its suburbs. In September 1976 a Buddhist monk arrived in the Thai capital from Singapore. It was Thanom Kittikachorn, who, as *Le Monde* (7–8 October 1976) observed, donned the orange robe of a Buddhist monk in order to create the conditions for a new military takeover without any great risk to himself.

Because he came with shaven head wearing the robe of a monk (having been ordained for the purpose) no one could, apparently, deny him entry. Students and staff of the universities protested against the return of the former dictator, and Thammasat University was occupied as part of this protest. On 6 October 1976 the students were attacked by armed gangs and subjected to hideous brutality. A group of American university teachers, in a letter to the *New York Times* dated 11 October 1976, writing 'as scholars, and in particular as Asian specialists', expressed 'shock at the brutal assault on Thammasat University in Bangkok, and at Thailand's renewed subjection to a military-dominated government'. The coup represented 'a violent reaction on the part of long-entrenched and authoritarian bureaucratic cliques to the "threatening" consequences of parliamentary democracy'; it was the overthrow of Thailand's first genuinely representative government by a regime which represented 'nothing but a discredited militarist past'.*

There were Buddhist monks from rural areas among those who during the brief period of democracy from 1973 to 1976 sought better conditions for the mass of Thailand's cultivators, for land rent in 1975 was as high as 50 per cent of the crop yield and loan interest stood at between 40 and 150 per cent (*Bangkok Post* 12 January 1975). But, while village Buddhist monks supported demands for reform, the royal monks of Bangkok appeared to have other loyalties. The return of Thanom as a monk met with no effective protest.

Thus, the close family links between monarchy and patriarchy

---

*The signatories were: Professors Benedict R. O. G. Anderson (Cornell), Jerome Alan Cohen (Harvard), George McT. Kahin (Cornell), Daniel S. Lev (Washington) and James C. Scott (Yale).

help to undergird the role of the king and Buddhism in Thailand as symbols which all must revere, at cost of being labelled 'communist'.

In post-war Burma the attempt to establish Buddhism as the state religion was made in 1961 by the pious Burmese Buddhist prime minister U Nu. We turn now to a brief account of this episode and its consequences.

U Nu, the promoter of Buddhism

U Nu became prime minister of Burma in 1947, on the eve of the country's independence from British rule. He accepted the office reluctantly, pressed as he was by the Governor, Sir Hubert Rance, to take this heavy responsibility at a time of great crisis. The crisis arose from the brutal murder on 19 July 1947 of the Burmese leader Bogyoke Aung San, who was to have headed the new government of Burma. With Aung San, six other executive councillors were also murdered. The massacre, which took place in the secretariat building as they sat in council, was carried out by gunmen acting under the orders of a political rival, U Saw. Sir Hubert Rance had been appointed in 1946 by the post-war Labour Government of Britain to go to Burma and work out a programme for handing over the control of Burma's affairs to the national leaders without delay. It was in these circumstances, following the deaths of seven members of the executive council, that Rance urged U Nu (who missed assassination because he had chanced to be absent that morning because of illness) to accept the task of forming and leading a new government. Seven years later U Nu recalled his mixed feelings of both reluctance and readiness. He had already been urged by one of his colleagues, Thakin Tin, to offer himself to the Governor as Aung San's successor, and he tells us that he 'did not hesitate a single moment. Yes, he would see the Governor and do what was required', with the provision, however, that 'with the expiry of six months after independence he would be allowed to resign' (75:133). But he seems to have acquired a taste for the job, and nineteen years later, when he was released from the imprisonment which in 1962 had ended his tragic and ineffectual attempt to lead the government of post-war Burma, he was still prepared to insist that he was 'legally' prime minister and to suggest that he should be immediately restored to office.

For our purposes it is appropriate to note his claims as a Buddhist, and in particular as 'promoter of the faith', a role in which, in the eyes of the Burmese people, he was continuing the traditions of Burma's Buddhist kings of the pre-British period. At the earliest opportunity after taking office as prime minister he turned his attention to his religious ambitions. According to one of his close friends he wished 'very much to go down in history as the leader who made Burma a Buddhist state again – a twentieth century Alaungpaya'. In keeping with this ambition was his own estimate of himself as a bodhisattva, a status which had been claimed also by some of the medieval Buddhist kings of Burma. U Nu had gradually developed an interest in Buddhist ideas, from having been originally what he has described as an 'hereditary Buddhist'. He records that he 'had never been properly instructed by a teacher in religious subjects, although he had done some reading and listened to lay preachers as well as learned monks'. He had, he says, only a 'little knowledge' (75:19). However, consciousness of his role as a bodhisattva was not inhibited by this. The 2,500th year of the Buddhist era was drawing near, and in popular imagination this was 'the time to long for the promoter of the Sāsana', the time when the ideal Buddhist ruler would appear. Popular imagination began to cast U Nu in this role (86:209). His authority in the eyes of the people was thus incomparably strengthened, and U Nu gracefully accepted the position which people ascribed to him. There was, perhaps, in Max Weber's phrase, an 'elective affinity' between being the ruler of Burma and the idea of being a bodhisattva, although U Nu would not have perceived it in these terms. Becoming virtually head of state encouraged his belief in himself as bodhisattva. Believing in himself as bodhisattva led him to wish to hold on to being head of state. Another aspect of the way in which personal Buddhist piety supported him in his public office was referred to˙by one of his colleagues, U Ba Swe, after the election of 1960: 'U Nu will sit in a pagoda for ten hours, if necessary, if he thinks it will help him politically' (12:67).

In 1950, therefore, when the more devastating political effects of the early post-war period has subsided a little, U Nu announced, in June of that year, that he was withdrawing for a period of meditation: 'My friends, I go to the Meditation Centre tomorrow. I have a vow to keep to attain the *thin – Khar – rupek – kha – nyan* [a stage in Buddhist meditation]. Until then do not send for me, even if the whole country is enveloped in flames. If there are fires, you must put them out yourselves' (75:195). Fortunately, as he himself adds, nothing serious happened before he attained this Buddhist objective, and that he did on 20 July.

The pace of political events having slackened enough to give him a breathing space, U Nu, as he himself records, 'began to think again about Buddhism, in which he was very interested [he refers to himself in the third person]. U Nu very much wanted the Buddhists to take advantage of the Buddha's teachings while they had the opportunity to do so. U Nu felt very unhappy when he found that the great majority of Buddhists had betrayed the privilege and opportunity to free themselves of endless suffering. With this thought he decided to (a) encourage interest in Buddhism, (b) disseminate the Law of Deliverance from suffering and (c) provide the facilities to achieve such deliverance through the practice of the prescribed disciplines' (75:196). The first official step that was taken was the passing by the Burma Government of the *Buddha Sasana* Organisation Act of 1950. The purpose of this was 'to organise the Promoters of the Faith into some kind of Parliament of *sasana* [religion]. All religious measures will be undertaken by the Union Parliament through the good offices of this Parliament of *sasana*' (109:169).

There then followed a programme for the development of Buddhism in Burma. This consisted of measures to deepen Buddhist understanding among monks and, in more elementary ways, among the lay people, and to spread Buddhism among the non-Buddhist inhabitants of the 'faraway hill tracts'. Monks were to have the opportunity to study in Pali 'universities' which were set up in certain monasteries. Examinations in Buddhist knowledge were arranged, mainly in knowledge of the Pali canonical scriptures, the *Tipitaka*. In order to establish the agreed authentic text of the *Tipitaka* a great synod was convened, to be held in Rangoon, the 'Sixth Buddhist Synod' as it was to be known. The previous one had been held at Mandalay in the reign of King Mindon, when the entire text of the *Tipitaka* had been inscribed on stone slabs. Mistakes in the carving of the text had made necessary a revision, and it so happened that the celebration in 1954 of the 2,500th year of the Buddhist era would provide a convenient occasion.

As far as the deepening of Buddhist knowledge among lay people was concerned U Nu himself took a lead by using 'what little knowledge he had', as he modestly puts it, 'to preach to audiences large and small'. He adds that 'if his text was needed for distribution he defrayed the printing costs as an act of charity'

(75:197). The *Tipitaka* was translated, so that those who did not understand Pali could read the scriptures in Burmese. Buddhist religious instruction was given in schools and to the students of Rangoon University and, most successfully, religious instruction was given to the inmates of jails; this proved very popular, as those who passed the test at the end of the course were let out of jail earlier. In order to provide opportunities for the practice by lay people of meditational disciplines U Nu established in Rangoon a Meditation Centre which he often visited. And in order to spread the knowledge of Buddhism, mainly in non-Buddhist areas of Burma, a Buddhist Missionary Society was founded with the financial backing of the government. Two aspects of this 'Frontier Buddhist Mission' are possibly significant, especially when compared with the efforts made in Thailand at the turn of the century to bring the hill people of the north fully into the institutional system of Bangkok Buddhism and the subsequent efforts to spread Buddhism in the potentially disaffected areas of north–east Thailand. First, the Mission was not based on the assumption that the hill areas of Burma were totally irreligious, for clearly this was not so. The hill people had their own traditional religious beliefs and practices, and some of them, especially the Kachins and Karens, for example, had become Christians. 'It is far from our intention', explained U Nu, 'to disparage in any way other religions like Mohammedanism, Hinduism, Christianity or spirit worship. We have been prompted by the sole consideration to combat effectively anti-religious forces which are rearing their ugly heads everywhere.' He then made it clear what forces he had in mind: 'It will be our duty to retort in no uncertain terms that the wisdom or knowledge that might be attributed to Karl Marx is less than one-tenth of a particle of dust that lies at the feet of our great Lord Buddha' (109:169f). Secondly, the Mission was directed, as in the Thai case, to the 'faraway hill tracts', in other words to the non-Burmese areas, where, among Karens, Kachins, Chins or Arakanese, some disaffection might be feared, especially if Communist agents were at work. In view of the known record of Chinese interference in Burma's affairs this was not an empty possibility (12:179, 254). The same kind of situation which in Thailand resulted in the Buddhist *Dhammaduta* programme (see pp.117f) had, in Burma under U Nu's government, produced an almost identical response.

In such enterprises as these U Nu saw himself as 'the promoter of the faith'. The fact that these enterprises also facilitated the proper governance of Burma, in his view of things, would not justify cynicism about his motives in undertaking them. Rather, the convergence of Buddhist interests and Burmese state interests would confirm his understanding of himself as a pious Buddhist ruler like Mindon (or Mongkut, or Chulalongkorn). The promotion of the faith was incomplete, however, until Buddhism had become the state religion of Burma. If there appeared to be a convergence between U Nu's Buddhist policies and those of neighbouring Thailand, that was not necessarily due to imitation by Burma or influence from Thailand: they both derived from the same Sinhalese Theravada archetypal form of state Buddhism. It is possible, however, that there was some conscious assimilation on U Nu's part, for during the 1950s he was on good terms with the Thai government. A border incident between the two countries in 1953 provided the occasion for U Nu to point out to his aggrieved colleagues, some of whom had been making angry speeches about Thai military provocation, that the record of past aggressive wars between the two countries did neither side credit and that it would be better 'to gain the friendship and goodwill of the Thais'. The following year, 1954, he had the opportunity, as guest at a dinner in Bangkok given by the head of the Thai government, Pibul Songgram, 'to say how much he deplored the frequent wars of the past between the Burmese and the Thais, and the attendant lootings and wanton destruction'. In 1955 Pibul Songgram visited Rangoon to take part in the ceremonies connected with the Sixth Buddhist Synod which U Nu had organised, and later that year U Nu visited the ruined city of Ayudhaya, destroyed by the Burmese in 1767. He went in company with Songgram and the two made an undertaking to build a new monastery and shrine there, with a new Buddha image. As a symbolic gesture the two heads of government planted a Bodhi tree in the sacred precinct. In 1960 the King and Queen of Thailand visited Burma; there were subsequent exchanges of cultural missions between the two countries, and U Nu's own summing up of the situation at the end of the fifties is that 'never before in history had the two countries been so well disposed towards each other' (75:271). This can be taken as, at any rate, an indication of U Nu's feelings towards Thailand at that time. It is not inconceivable that his visits to this neighbouring Buddhist state and the euphoric attitude towards Thailand and its affairs which they had engendered played some part in influencing his view of the relationship which should exist between government and religion in a Buddhist country.

The 1950s were characterised pre-eminently, so far as Buddhism was concerned, as the period of preparation for and celebration of the 2,500th year of Buddhist era, the 'Buddha-Jayanti'. In Burma this was the occasion, as we have noted, for the holding of the Sixth Buddhist Synod. Primarily concerned with the revision and codification of the Pali canonical texts, and therefore attended by Buddhist representatives from all over Burma and from Thailand, Laos, Cambodia, Ceylon and elsewhere, the Council provided a stimulus to the Buddhists of Burma particularly. The proceedings of the Council, which lasted for two years, were held in a vast, specially constructed artificial 'cave' at Kaba Aye, on the outskirts of Rangoon, which, after the Council had ended on the full moon day of May 1956 (the 2,500th anniversary, it is alleged, of the Buddha's decease, or *parinibbana*), remained, together with the adjacent 'Peace Pagoda', as visible assertions of the idea that Burma had served as the centre of the Buddhist world; in continuance of this role an international Buddhist study centre was established there which attracted scholars from Asian and Western countries, Mahayana as well as Theravada.

There was also a belief among Burmese Buddhists, a belief which U Nu referred to in a speech which he made in India two years before the celebrations began, that the Buddha Jayanti year would 'be the most auspicious since the spread of the Lord Buddha's teachings began'. Commenting on this, Hugh Tinker adds the note that many Burmans believe that the Lord Buddha charged Sakya (Pali, Sakka, the head of the gods) 'to assume sovereignty over the world on the 2,500th anniversary of his decease: Sakya was empowered to reward the virtuous and punish the wicked'. This idea influenced many people in Burma to support the Buddhist revival which U Nu was trying to bring about and to contribute to the preparations for the Sixth Council (109:173).

One of the aspects of the 'revival' was a new aggressiveness on the part of some of the monks of Burma. Michael Mendelson has warned those who engage in the study of Buddhist Burma against making indiscriminate reference to 'the monks', as though they were a united and uniform community speaking with one voice. There are many sectional interests among the bhikkhus, or 'pongyis', of Burma. The more aggressively inclined section has, in recent years, gained a good deal of attention, simply because they are more vociferous than others. Some of these came to U Nu in 1954 with a complaint. Addressing him as 'Dagagyi', that is 'benefactor' (of the Buddhist religion), they made their complaint in the following direct and unambiguous terms, recorded by U Nu himself:

'Dagagyi, we've come to object to Islam and Christianity being taught in state schools. We want this stopped immediately.'
'Monks, why do you dislike those subjects?'
'Because they are heresies.'
'Only Moslems study Islam, and Christians Christianity. Buddhist students do not study them.'
'Don't have them taught in state schools. If they want to study these subjects, let them go elsewhere.'
'Please refrain from injustice. King Mindon was a great patron of the Buddhist religion. During his reign he gave considerable aid to the Christian and Moslem faiths in his capital, Mandalay.'
'We were not there in Mindon's reign. Had we been present we would have prevented such aid.'
'State schools are run not only with money provided by the Buddhists, but with taxes paid also by Moslems and Christians. If therefore Buddhism is to be taught in these schools, equal opportunity must be given Islam and Christianity.'
'We most strongly object. These subjects shall not be taught.' (75 : 200).

U Nu's response to what he perceived as 'a majority group cold-bloodedly trying to suppress minority groups' was to dismiss them curtly, with the assurance that if Islam and Christianity were not to be taught no other religious subjects would be taught either. This decision of U Nu's, when reported in the newspapers, caused an uproar. U Nu, however, refused to be browbeaten and, on a visit to Mandalay, released an even more inflammatory statement to the press. On his return to Rangoon he found a deputation of Muslim leaders waiting to see him. They told him that the Muslim community in Rangoon now feared for their safety, as the rumour had been put about that U Nu's decision on the subject of withdrawing Buddhist religious teaching in schools had been instigated by the Muslims. At once, he offered to call a press conference and take full personal responsibility for the decision. The following exchange between the Muslim leaders and U Nu then took place:

'No, Mr. Prime Minister, please don't do that. A press conference would be powerless to help. Rumours have moved things too far. The robbers and looters are inciting the people to riot. Only this afternoon, a group of monks and their followers entered our street and threatened us. They called us pork-eating mother-fornicators and proclaimed we would be turned into corpses.'

'Then what do you expect me to do?'

'Please withdraw your order and meet the monks' demands. It is of no great importance that we cannot teach Islam in state schools. We can make other arrangements.'

U Nu records that he spent a sleepless night, tortured by visions of Buddhist-Muslim riots in Rangoon like those of 1938 (see pp. 88f). In the end, he gave in, and accepted the intolerant demands of the Buddhist monks (75:203f).

This incident illustrates the kind of chauvinism which could find expression in the mid-1950s within the general context of an officially encouraged Buddhist revival. It illustrates also the kind of apprehension which was felt not only by Muslims, but by other non-Burmese-Buddhist minorities such as the Karens, the Shans, the Kachins and the Chins. As they saw it the dominant Burmese-speaking community was intending to impose a cultural hegemony upon all subjects of the Rangoon government. Some were already in political revolt against the government, and some (such as the Karens) continued in revolt throughout the 1950s. Others, not until 1960 in open political revolt, were alienated by the proposal put forward by U Nu in the election campaign that year to make Buddhism the state religion of Burma.

It might seem that in making this proposal U Nu was acting inconsistently. Having tried to insist that Buddhists should *not* enjoy the special privilege of being allowed a monopoly of religious instruction, he was now, it seemed, insisting that Buddhists *should* be in a special position in the Republic of Burma, in that theirs was to be the official religion of the state. The fact appears to be that U Nu's policies over the period of his premiership were not always consistent. As Butwell observes, in 1947 U Nu advocated socialism as a means of enabling men to practise Buddhism more effectively. But by 1957 he was advocating Buddhism as the means of making socialism possible, on the familiar grounds that 'you cannot change economic systems until you first change human hearts'. By 1959 he was once again advocating his original view: the reason why the average Buddhist was not seeking the ultimate goal of release from *Samsara* was that the economic system predisposed him to seek other, materialistic goals; hence, if the economic system were changed, men would be able to pursue Buddhist aims more readily (12:72). These apparent oscillations of view are, of course, explicable as changes of emphasis according to the audience being addressed. When (in 1947 and 1959) he was addressing those who had to be persuaded of the desirability of socialism he presented it as a means to the attainment of Buddhist ends. When he was addressing those who had to be persuaded of the value of Buddhism he presented it as a means of achieving socialist ends. At other times he has commended Buddhism for its power (as he saw it) to strengthen the 'moral fibre of the nation'. In the end one is forced back to the view that looking for consistent principles in U Nu's public utterances is not a very profitable exercise.

Buddhism as the state religion of Burma

Having chided Buddhist monks for their intolerance of the other religions of Burma, U Nu nevertheless himself made his promise to establish Buddhism as the state religion one of the main issues of the election campaign of early 1960. His own account of the matter is as follows:

> Out of his abundant religious zeal, U Nu had for a long time been desirous of making Buddhism the state religion. He knew that if he did so Burma would not be the only country in the world where the religion professed by the majority was made the state religion. Moreover, he sincerely believed that equitable adjustments could be made in order to ensure that the state religion did not become an instrument for imposing a tyranny of the majority. As a result, during the campaign for the 1960 general elections, U Nu made a commitment that if his party won he would make Buddhism the state religion (75:204).

His party did win, by a handsome majority, and U Nu was faced with the necessity of fulfilling his promise. He began by sounding out the opinion of the minorities: Muslim, Hindu, Christian,

Shan, Karen, and Kachin. He pointed out that freedom of worship for all was already safeguarded by the Constitution, Article 21 (3) of which read, 'The State shall not impose any disabilities or make any discrimination on the ground of religious faith or belief'. Apparently U Nu sincerely believed, or hoped to persuade others to believe, that making Buddhism the state religion would be compatible with not imposing disabilities or making discrimination against non-Buddhist citizens. The minorities, however, were not persuaded.

There was strong opposition from the minorities to the proposed Act for making Buddhism the state religion; a National Religious Minorities alliance was formed, representing all the non-Buddhists of Burma. On the whole the resistance they organised was peaceful, but there was a high degree of tension in the capital on 26 August, 1961, the date the Act was passed by the two houses of Burma's parliament. The usually crowded streets were deserted for fear of the violence which might erupt, and armoured vehicles stood waiting near the parliament building for the trouble which, as it happened, did not come. A week later, speaking in the Chamber of Deputies, U Nu warned his fellow Buddhists of the tenseness of the situation. He pointed out that 'laws alone cannot prevent the fears of non-Buddhists from materialising. It is necessary for the hundreds of thousands of Buddhists to attain the right view and to restrain themselves in speech, act and thought in all matters which concern non-Buddhists' (12:225).

Some of the Christians then pointed out that the Constitution did not specifically give them the right to *teach* their religion, but only to believe and practise it. They asked that mention of the right to teach should, therefore, be introduced into the Constitution. This U Nu promised he would do. As soon as his promise became publicly known the militant Buddhist monks voiced their opposition to the proposal and demanded the postponement of the amendment to some later time. U Nu had emphasised the moral duty of Buddhists, the majority community, to act with tolerance now that their religion was state established, but the response had been a renewed outburst of hostility from the militant monks' organisation. At a less violent level, however, there was disquiet among Buddhists over the proposal to give Christians the right to teach Christian doctrines in their schools. It was felt that this might provide a loophole for Christian missionary propaganda to be directed against Buddhist and Muslim pupils in Christian schools. An additional clause was therefore introduced, providing that no pupil should be taught any religion other than that of his parents without their written consent. The monks' organisations protested that 'the sins' of the amendment now being brought before Parliament 'would greatly outweigh the merits of making Buddhism the state religion' (96:272). The matter was thus conceived and expressed in Theravada Buddhist religious terms: Sin and merit. On these religious doctrinal grounds a matter of national, public policy was being argued. Extremely worded statements were issued by the Buddhist leaders from mass meetings at which the atmosphere was charged with 'fever-pitch emotionalism'; the organisers declared that the members of the Buddhist Sangha were in a state of mental agony such 'as if they had been bitten on the head by a snake' (96:275). It is possible here to give only a brief impression of the nature of this bitter Buddhist opposition, when any expression of moderation was a voice crying in the wilderness. But it is this wild fanaticism of the organised Buddhist monks, described at length in chapter seven of D. E. Smith's book, which has to be kept in mind when the attitude of General Ne Win and his government to the monks is considered (96).

Various factors had by the beginning of March 1962 combined to bring U Nu's regime to a close. They have been identified as 'dissension and division in U Nu's Union Party; the promulgation of Buddhism as the state religion; the rise of insurrectionary activity, particularly among the [Karens] and other minorities'; new demands for federalism, especially from the Shans; and U Nu's generally ineffective handling of the situation; 'he exhorted and temporised while disunity spread' (112:291f). These factors were interconnected, and prominent among the causes of the disquiet felt by the minorities was, undoubtedly, the making of Buddhism the state religion. It was not itself the most important cause of disunity within the Republic of Burma, but it served to emphasise the disquiet felt by the non-Burmese and and non-Buddhist communities and to aggravate resentment against what was felt to be Burmese Buddhist dominance. In a coup swiftly and easily carried out in the early hours of 2 March 1962, the Burmese army, under General Ne Win, took over the government of the country. In a press conference a few days later Ne Win explained: 'In Burma we had economic, religious and political crises with the issue of federalism the most important reason for the *coup* . . . A small country like Burma cannot afford divisions', if it wished to avoid sinking like Vietnam (12:240).

Ne Win, himself a Buddhist, had no hesitation in reversing the amendment to the Constitution which had made Buddhism the state religion. He also abandoned some of the traditional but now archaic social practices which U Nu had encouraged as expressions of Burma's 'Buddhist' ethos. Nevertheless the new regime, when it came to work out a philosophy and a national programme, gave an important place to Buddhist values. 'These values are both individual and social. They readily support a grass-roots democratic social structure. The regime clearly recognised the "spiritual" in life based on its Buddhist analysis of the interacting "material", "animal" and "phenomenal" worlds (respectively *okasaloka, sattaloka, sankharaloka)*' (113:210f). Moreover, the regime's adherence to the Buddhist doctrine of ceaseless change *(paticca-samuppada)*, in which it sees an affinity to the Marxian 'dialectic', leads it to view its own programme and ideology as open to constant amendment and alteration. Frank Trager sees 'the regime's special emphasis on and support for peasant proprietorship and co-operative undertakings' as another 'affirmation of traditional Burmese beliefs and values' (112:211). It is necessary to understand that what is meant by 'traditional Burmese' is the traditional Burmese Buddhism of village life and the kind of values which characterised Burmese rural society described earlier in this chapter. The contrast and indeed the tension which existed for centuries between what can be called royal Buddhism – the religion of the king and the court – and village Buddhism has perhaps been glimpsed from time to time in the course of this historical survey. Royal Buddhism belongs inseparably to that period of history when monarchy was a common form of government, still acceptable to the majority of people; it is therefore less appropriate in the modern world. U Nu had tried to reverse history and to re-establish in the twentieth century a patched up version of royal Buddhism. In doing so he jeopardised Burma's development as a modern religiously plural state, and thereby its general development. Ne Win and his government, on the other hand, in rejecting such blatant and irrelevant traditionalism were not rejecting Buddhism or its values, especially as these are expressed in the lives of the great mass of the village people of Burma.

From time to time throughout the history of Burma and Thailand royal Buddhism has invaded the lives of the people, making demands upon them and pressing them into the service of an expansionist and even imperialistic ruler. Village Buddhism and its values were then overridden by royal Buddhism and its by no means compatible values. In order to make clearer this tension which has thus existed within both Burmese and Thai Buddhism it may be profitable by way of a conclusion to this short study to consider the issues which are entailed in the record of Buddhist nations at war.

6

Buddhists at War

The religion of peace

One sometimes encounters the notion that Buddhism is a religion of peace. In certain respects it is so, for its doctrines give a high place to the efficacy of *ahimsa*, or non-violence, in solving human problems. But we have to consider also whether it can be called a religion of peace in the sense that those countries which have large numbers of Buddhists (by self-definition) can be shown to have a high rate of peaceableness in their relations with one another and with non-Buddhist countries. Some Buddhists have claimed that this is the case. In 1950 Burma's Attorney-General, U Chan Htoon, asserted that 'Buddhism is the only *ideology* which can give peace to the world and save it from war and destruction. . . . For that reason the peoples of the world are looking to Buddhism to save the world'. In a similar vein U Nu claimed that 'Unlike the theistic creeds [Buddhism] cannot sanction (even) such acts of violence that are necessary for the preservation of public order and society' (86:221). This was also one of the reasons why U Nu believed that Buddhism was incompatible with Marxism. On the other hand, U Ba Swe, another post-war Burmese leader, in a speech entitled 'The Pattern of the Burmese Revolution', given to trade union leaders in Rangoon in December 1951, expressed the view that Marxist theory and Buddhist philosophy were compatible, and also made it clear that a revolutionary programme based on these two was very appropriate for Burma; while a peaceful solution to Burma's problem would be desirable, nevertheless if those problems could only be solved by force he personally would have no qualms in using force. The record of the Buddhist kingdoms of

Burma and Thailand indicates that U Ba Swe was more accurately representing the Buddhist position in these matters than were U Nu or U Chan Htoon.

The historical record of the Buddhist kingdoms of South–East Asia does not support the view that where Buddhist institutions and ideas have a prominent place in national life the consequence will be peaceful international relations. Nor is there any clear evidence that in countries where Buddhism is the state religion national wars have been regarded as un-Buddhistic activities. The evidence suggests, on the contrary, that Buddhism in South–East Asia has been successfully employed to reinforce the policies and interests of national rulers, often in their competition with one another for resources or prestige. Burma and Thailand provide excellent examples in this respect.

A Thai Buddhist apologia for military virtues

At the coronation of King Rama VI of Thailand in the year 1910 the Buddhist Patriarch delivered a discourse on the three qualities of (1) desire for righteousness *(dhammakāmata)*; (2) desire for the welfare of others *(atthakāmata)*; and (3) the policy of governance *(ratthābhipānopāya)*. First, those who considered only their own personal convenience were contrasted with those who were firm in righteousness and the performance of their duties, and ready and willing to 'sacrifice their lives for the sake of their religion and their country'. His Majesty was congratulated on the fact that he was 'always full of desire for Righteousness and steadfast in Righteousness', an example to all. Touching the second point, desire for the welfare of others, the Patriarch again assured His Majesty that he always directed affairs of state in a smooth manner, and that this virtuous quality would bring prosperity and stability to the Buddhist Sangha and the Kingdom of Thailand.

Thirdly, as to the policy of governance, cognisance had to be taken of the fact, said the Patriarch, that 'people who live in different countries in close neighbourhood must inevitably have disputes and quarrels, either on account of territory, or of the rights of the subjects thereof, or of commercial rivalry, and so forth . . . Such being the case, each nation finds it necessary to organise some of its own citizens into a class whose duty it is to fight against its enemies.' The preacher quoted the Ksatriya class of ancient India, with the king as the chief Ksatriya, as a case in point. He then went on to say that 'defence against external foes is one of the policies of governance and is one that cannot be neglected'. War, he pointed out, usually occurs suddenly, and a country must therefore always be prepared. 'Wars must be prepared for even in time of peace, otherwise one would not be in time, and one would be in a disadvantageous position towards one's foe.' He quoted some words of the Buddha in support of this: 'As a town situated on the frontier must be prepared internally and externally, so too should you be prepared.' Thailand, he continued, had 'enjoyed great prosperity because all her citizens used to be warriors.' But now civilians and the military had become separate classes. The civilians, he lamented, had 'become totally inexperienced in warfare, and even the military were none too proficient'. Now, however, things were changing; and he congratulated His Majesty on the measures he had recently taken to promote the welfare of the army. He had also begun to improve the navy. He had founded the Corps of Wild Tigers. And, Your Majesty, he continued, 'You have initiated among schoolboys the Boy Scout Movement to foster in boys the warrior spirit'. All this, he considered, was evidence of the king's desire to turn his people into warriors as of old, and thus evidence of the king's wise attention to the policy of governance. So great had his fame in this direction become, the Patriarch reminded him, that His Majesty King George V of Great Britain and Ireland had come to hear of it, and had asked His Majesty to accept the rank of honorary General in the British Army, an honour never before bestowed upon any other sovereign in the Orient. The sermon concluded with pious birthday wishes for His Majesty's continued prosperity, success, happiness and long life, and an invocation to the guardian angels of the Kingdom of Siam to be benevolent and keep watch over him, granting him his pious wishes and guarding him from all evil.

The preface to the printed edition of this sermon urges the reader to remember that it is 'an erroneous idea to suppose that the Buddha condemned all wars and people whose business it was to wage war'. What the Buddha condemned was the spirit miscalled 'militarism', which is 'really intolerant and unreasoning hatred, vengeance and savagery which causes men to kill from sheer blood-lust'.

Buddhist kings and military conquest

It has to be remembered that the sermon was preached in the

year 1916. The First World War was at its height, and this formed an important element in the background to the occasion; the preacher at one point explicitly mentioned 'the present Great War in Europe' as an example of how 'even though the world had grown so civilised' people prefer, instead of asking a third party to arbitrate between two parties in a dispute, to use their own strength to decide issues. In 1916 the Thai army had not fired any shots in anger worth mentioning for over fifty years, in fact not since Thai troops marched into Cambodia to annex the western part of that country to Thailand in 1861–2.

It might therefore be thought that the emphasis given by King Vajiravudh to military discipline and the need for military preparedness was an aberration in the history of Buddhist Thailand and was due to the combination of two circumstances: the context of World War and the fact that Thailand has a king who had been trained as a British army officer. A moment's reflection will show that this would be a misjudgement. Thailand was not in any military danger in 1916. King Vajiravudh, as an Anglophile, strongly supported England and France, by his extensive journalistic writings and with gifts of money to his old regiment, the Durham Light Infantry. Eventually, in July 1917, Thailand entered the war and a small volunteer expeditionary force, about 1,200 strong, went to Europe under a Thai major-general. They arrived too late to take much part in the actual fighting, but were able to join in the victory parades in Paris and London, and later in Bangkok.

The fact that Thailand's king had undergone a military training was not an accident of history. This Buddhist prince, Vajiravudh, did not drift into an army career: he chose it, and he enjoyed the life. Even when he left Sandhurst and went up to Oxford he read history, he chose to write a dissertation on the subject of 'The War of Polish Succession'. Clearly, military matters fascinated him. As soon as he came down from Oxford he went to the School of Musketry at Hythe and obtained a special certificate for marksmanship (99:155f). This fascination which wars and armies had for Vajiravudh is fully in keeping with the tradition of many centuries.

Buddhist kings in Thailand, Burma, Cambodia, and Laos (to name no others) had throughout the history of these nations been much concerned with their armed forces not only as instruments of national defence but also for conquest and expansion. From the Burmese king Anawrahta's campaign of expansion in

Mon territory in the eleventh century onwards, the list of battle honours gained by the armies of the many Buddhist kingdoms is one which would not disgrace such great shrines of military glory as Canterbury Cathedral or Westminster Abbey. As occasion demanded, and sometimes when it did not, Burmese fought Mons, and Pyus, and Thais, and Laos. Similarly the Thais fought the Laos, and the Malays, and the Khmers and the Burmese. The story is a long one, with some more notable moments, such as the unscrupulous massacre carried out by the Burmese at Pegu, and their savage and complete destruction and burning of the beautiful Thai capital city of Ayudhaya in 1767. The Thais for their part had on various occasions attempted to conquer large parts of eastern and southern Burma, and before that had expanded their kingdom far southwards from Sukhodaya into the Malayan peninsula. The Burmese Alaungpaya dynasty had cherished dreams of empire stretching far beyond the western borders of Burma towards India, and in the eighteenth century their armies occupied not only the southern parts of Bengal and Manipur but advanced far into Assam and occupied the Brahmaputra valley. It was, from the Burmese point of view, unfortunate that this very promising empire-building campaign of the late eighteenth century brought them into conflict with what was at that time another large and, as it turned out, superior empire-building nation, namely Britain.

These were not wars of religion. More often than not the armed forces of Buddhist kings in Indochina were fighting those of other Buddhist kings; but occasionally, when necessary, they would fight Hindus, or Muslims, or Christians. There was no religious partiality about them. They would fight men of any religion or of none, if opportunity or the occasion demanded it.

The same has been true, in turn, of the armed forces of kings and rulers adhering to other faiths – Muslims, Hindus and Christians. As V. G. Kiernan has put it recently, 'Every type of society in history has had its characteristic pattern of aggressiveness' (47). All have been aggressive, and either all shall have prizes for their aggression or all alike should certainly be exonerated from religious discrimination. That is to say there seems to be no justification for regarding one religious tradition as characteristically much more strongly associated with military aggression and another as more strongly associated with peace. Muslims have fought not only Christians, Jews, Hindus and Zoroastrians; they have also fought other Muslim nations, on many occasions (the most recent example being the war of 1971 between Pakistan and Bangladesh). The armies of Christian Europe have fought not only Turks, Hindus, Buddhists and other varieties of 'heathen'; they have, and possibly even more frequently, fought one another – French, English, German, Spanish, Dutch, Greek and so on. Hindu kingdoms have not been high in the charts for this sort of thing for some centuries now, but they had a good record once, and as recently as 1769 a Hindu regime from Rajputana conquered the territory along the lower slopes of the central Himalayas and created the modern state of Nepal, whose population subsequently became a source of excellent recruits for the British Army.

The point to note is this: that the incidence of international warfare bears no positive correlation to the dominance, or absence, of any one religious tradition. The *causes* of international conflicts are to be found mainly in the realm of material interest, as the Patriarch said in his sermon; on account of territory, or the rights of subjects or commercial rivalry, and so forth. Sometimes perhaps they are to be found in the realm of psychology. This is not to say, however, that the *reasons* given by those who launch wars will not sometimes be couched in ideological or, if you like, religious terms, like making the world safe for democracy or, in the case of the military conquests which brought the British Empire into existence, so that, as it was once said, 'We might carry on with better effect the great work of the world's conversion from darkness to light, and from the power of Satan unto God' (29:6). A German statesman once complimented Britain, France and Russia as colony-owners on their ability in this respect; they showed outstanding skill, he observed, at 'cloaking practical motives and instincts in high sounding words which make them seem beautiful' (11:320). But these were the *reasons* handed out whenever it seemed politic to do so; they were not the *causes* of British, French and other forms of European military aggression; the causes were in some sense or other material, namely the defence of interests such as those of the East India Company, a body of men who had so little regard for religious expansion that they positively forbade Christian missionaries to operate in their territory, in Bengal for example, until they were required by the British Government at Westminster to adopt a different policy. This can be seen as a *quid pro quo*, the Company having, like other financial interests of that period, 'hauled the political and military power of their governments behind them' (47:2).

But in many of the cases of military conquest carried out by Buddhist kings it was these kings themselves who had initiated the aggressive action. This suggests the possibility that the understanding of national aggression might be aided by an inquiry into the nature of personal aggression in a Buddhist society. It will be possible to do so in only a brief and summary fashion, but perhaps some tentative conclusions will be possible, of a kind which will help to explain why two Buddhist nations at least, Burma and Thailand, have been so warlike.

Non-aggression in interpersonal behaviour

In Burmese and Thai society one of the chief characteristics of interpersonal behaviour is the avoidance of aggression. In Burma the most admired type of personality is called *lein hmade lu,* that is one who 'avoids fights and arguments, never uses harsh words, and states things so that hearers get the point easily' (72:270). Stating things clearly is necessary in order to avoid misunderstandings, with possible consequent hostility; perhaps there is also a sense of the unwisdom of affecting an aloof manner suggestive of the superiority of one who says 'Of course, you cannot understand these things; you are not as wise as I.' Such an attitude is studiously to be avoided, in the view of the Burmese Buddhist; one should attempt to make one's meaning clear and always be willing to communicate openly. The man who has lived successfully is the man who has exemplified this ideal personality, and who has not quarrelled with his neighbours and has exhibited *lein hmade'.* Such a person becomes known as *lugyi lugaun,* which can be loosely translated as 'an outstandingly good man' (72:270).

Even although the majority of people may not achieve this kind of status, all will seek to order their conduct in ways which will at least enable them to avoid incurring the displeasure of others. A common Burmese saying which expresses this attitude is *Be jaun amon hkanyamale?* ('Why should I incur hatred by speaking out?') (72:271). The general gist of this and similar common sayings is, Why stir people up and make them angry with you? Live quietly and avoid upsetting people.

By way of compensation for such restraint, however, a great deal of gossip is indulged in. As Manning Nash puts it: 'The contrast between the delicacy and smoothness of inter-personal behaviour and the *atin pyawde* (behind-the-back talk) is stark' (72:271).

A strikingly similar account of Thai interpersonal behaviour emerges from Herbert Phillips's study of Bang Chang. 'The most obvious fact about aggression in Bang Chang', says Phillips, 'is that villagers cannot tolerate its spontaneous, direct expression in face to face relationships.' This is demonstrated, he says, 'not only by the general absence of overt aggression in such relationships but by the elaborate array of devices that villagers use to control its expression: giggling when making or receiving an untoward request, using a go-between to soften the demand of an inter-personal lien, leaving the field at the slightest hint of provocation (whether the provocation is intended or not), as well as the more general use of flattery, comedy, and self-effacement' (79:184).

Anyone who has lived in Burma or Thailand is likely to agree that the predominant quality felt in personal encounters is of mildness and amiability. As Phillips puts it, face-to-face contacts have 'an aura of surface pleasantness, but', he adds, 'at the same time a high degree of brittleness'. He cites one of many similar cases of a villager who explained that he and his friend are on good terms because they never disagree on anything. 'We never never disagree. Only people who are drunkards and take opium disagree.'

Phillips lists three ways in which Thai villagers vent their feelings, as alternatives to expressing aggression directly. The first is really nasty gossip about the object of their hostile feelings. In an aside he comments that Thailand just as appropriately as being called 'Land of Smiles' could be called 'Land of Gossip'. The same is certainly true of Burma; one is there very much aware of an all-pervading atmosphere of gossip in which all are involved. (It is interesting that the same is said to be true of another Buddhist community, the Tibetans.) The second, and only slightly less common, method of venting hostile feelings in Thailand is by calculated acts or utterances of what Phillips calls 'ritual aggression', such as 'when someone calls a dog by the name of a person who is within hearing range and claims it was simply a slip of the tongue'. In retaliation the victim 'might respond by stealing his antagonist's boat and returning it a few weeks later, after his adversary had suffered sufficient anxiety' (79:186). The third and much less common way of venting hostile feelings is that of magical aggression, that is the use of witchcraft and magical practices to harm somebody towards whom hostility is felt.

In all this one thing becomes clear: that Thai (and Burmese) Buddhists are well aware of the potential they all possess for feeling hostility towards others. But they are equally convinced that ways should be found of avoiding its direct and open expression. Why they should be so concerned to control aggression can be explained in a number of ways.

One is that they have been taught, and have accepted, that *dosa* (enmity) is one of the three fundamental roots of evil and of suffering, and that enmity is never overcome by enmity; enmity is overcome only by non-enmity. It has to be acknowledged that while interpersonal relations in Thailand and Burma imply acknowledgement of the first half of this saying from the Dhammapada, the second half containing the recommended solution is not so often resorted to; rather alternative, less dangerous ways of venting hostile feelings are found. The explanation suggested by Phillips on the basis of his fieldwork is that the Thais' aggression control derives from a generalised fear of losing equilibrium, or of becoming psychically disassembled, if they vent their anger openly. He suggests also that in controlling their aggression they are aware of keeping their psychic problems to themselves and not implicating others in them, and that this is a manifestation of respect for others. On the other hand, he acknowledges, there may in many cases simply be a straightforward fear of the painful consequences in terms of reprisals if they were to release their anger. He sums this up by saying 'rather than work out their aggressions behaviorally – in and with other human beings – they work them out in the isolation of their own inner psychodynamics' (79:188).

Another context in which aggression control may be seen is that of the hierarchy of power, in Burmese *hpon*. The most powerful beings in the Burman villager's universe are the *nats* or spirits; in Thailand the corresponding concept is *phi*. There are great nats and little nats (in Burmese, *athet* and *auk*, upper and lower). It is mostly the latter, nearer to the earth, that the villager has to watch out for, and propitiate when necessary. The most prominent among them, it will be recalled, are the Thirty-Seven, whose leader is a *nat* named Min Maha Giri, the Prince of the Great Mountain, known in Burmese as Einzaung Nat. Many of the nats are spirits of men who died violent deaths, by murder or by drowning for instance. They are, on the whole, not well disposed towards humans, but their hostility can be appeased if men show them proper respect and make appropriate offerings. The whole landscape is swarming with them, and a man has to take very good care at all times not to offend one of them. June Nash records that 'negligent as the average village woman is about her housekeeping duties' the only thing she ever heard neighbours criticise was a woman's failure to propitiate the nats. She observes also that nobody she met, not even the most devoted meditator, 'was so foolhardy as to risk the anger of a nat' (71:127).

This extreme respect which the villager shows towards the nats in order not to incur displeasure is strikingly similar to his attitude in interpersonal relations. June Nash remarks on this parallel: 'Wives show the same consideration to their husbands; one woman said that having a husband is like having a *nat* in the house – he must be cared for, deferred to, and any impingements upon his *hpon*, or male power, must be avoided' (71:129). Children also tend to be appeased as one would appease nats, attempting to meet their wishes and not to frustrate them. She makes this most significant comment: 'The avoidance of conflict and the consideration for the sentiments and interests of others evident in the treatment in *nats* is a characteristic of all social interaction, expressed in the term *a nade* (71:129).

The Burmese expression *a nade* is very widely used and is difficult to render into English. Manning Nash explains it as follows:

> *A nade* always comes up in social situations. One does not feel *a nade* when an action or idea involves no others. *A nade* is consequent on interaction between status unequals and is absent from the most intimate, full, personal interaction and largely inoperative among peers and age mates . . . the operation of *a nade* prevents a sharply defined emotional situation, a blazing argument, a direct contradiction, a clash of persons . . . (72:269).

As one avoids conflict with nats, so, by the operation of *a nade*, one avoids conflict between persons. In both cases there is a sense of status inequality; in both cases there is the fear of provoking an acute and painful reaction. It seems to me that there is here another possible source of the *general* attitude of *lein hmade* – avoidance of fights and arguments. Once established as a proper attitude towards nats and status superiors, whose hostile actions, when provoked, could not be withstood, the same attitude might very easily be extended to anyone else, even if he were not formally one's status superior, for he too might react with unpleasant violence. The successful man in the Burmese and Thai view is he who manages to steer his way carefully through life, avoiding dangerous encounters with the hostile spirits which lurk everywhere and can all too easily be provoked. By extension, the successful man is also he who proceeds with similar caution in all his interpersonal encounters. The origin of this mode of conduct might, therefore, be seen in the cult of nats as much as in Buddhist morality.

Royal aggression

There was, however, one man who had no status superiors, at least none within his own kingdom, and that was the king. The king was, in traditional Burmese and Thai thought, a being apart from other men, virtually a god, only to be approached prostrate and with the use of the most exaggerated of honorific forms of address. The only challenge of this godlike status a Buddhist king would be likely to encounter would be from another Buddhist king. Whose *hpon* was the superior might then have to be decided in the only way possible, by combat. If, as was usually the case, strong material considerations had precipitated the encounter, all the considerations which operate at the level of ordinary mortal men's interpersonal behaviour to inhibit aggression would here be non-existent; there would be no reason why open aggression should be avoided.

When this kind of situation arose, as it seems to have done often enough in Burmese and Thai history, the state of war between the two kings would be implemented by calling upon each local or provincial ruler in the kingdom to provide from his region a quota of men and arms. There were no standing armies worthy of the name before the nineteeenth century; armed forces were recruited as occasion demanded. Sangermano described the situation as it still existed in eighteenth-century Burma as follows:

> The soldiery in the Burmese Empire is on a very different footing from ours: it does not consist of regiments of soldiers with various ensigns, who live separately from other members

of society in barracks, castles and fortresses, without wives and children, and exercise no other trade but that of handling arms, and going through warlike exercises. Those who in this country perform military service are the whole Burmese nation, who in quality of slaves of the Emperor, and whenever he commands them, are obliged to take arms (85:97).

The troops thus enlisted would have had no special training and could not have inherited any codes of what was good regimental behaviour, any *esprit de corps*, or any regard for the military value of discipline. Sangermano says:

...destitute as these people are of discipline and of all knowledge of tactics, they never can be said to engage in a regular battle, but merely to skirmish under the protection of trees or palisades; or else they approach the hostile town or army under the cover of a mound of earth, which they throw up as they advance. It may indeed sometimes happen that two parties will meet in the open plain, but without any method or order; one endeavours either to surround the other or to gain its rear, and thus put it to flight. But it is when they enter without resistance an enemy's country that they show their true spirit; which, while it is most vile and dastardly in danger, is proportionately proud and cruel in victory. The crops, the houses, the convents of Talapoins are all burnt to the ground, the fruit trees are cut down, and all the unfortunate inhabitants, who may fall into their hands, murdered without distinction (85:99).

The following conclusions can therefore be suggested:
1 The avoidance of aggression in interpersonal behaviour in Thai and Burmese society can be regarded as having its roots partly in the canonical doctrines of Theravada regarding *ahimsa*, the evil nature and consequence of *dosa*, and the importance of *adosa* or *metta* in acquiring good karma. The *nat* and *phi* cults and the attitudes of carefulness in the face of superior power and avoidance of aggression which these cults instil into ordinary people also serve to support the orthodox Buddhist doctrines and these have, therefore, survived without difficulty.
2 The effect of such control of aggression and avoidance of release of anger in interpersonal relations is, as Phillips suggests, to cause the members of such societies to work out their aggres-

sions (of whose reality and potential they are well aware) in what he calls 'the isolation of their own inner psycho-dynamics'.
3   This has applied to all except the king, for whom such carefulness and deference would be inappropriate. Occasions when aggressive emotions in a king are likely to be dangerous are limited to when his will comes into conflict with that of another king. In such a case, and for such a person, open aggression is countenanced in Thai and Burmese Buddhism and regarded as proper.
4   The ordinary men who, from their villages all over the kingdom, are then enlisted into the service of the king are, as we have seen, men whose personal feelings of aggression are not being given open expression but are being dealt with either indirectly and incompletely in gossip, or, still incompletely, in their own individual inner psycho-dynamics. In the situation of war against an enemy kingdom they are allowed a release, in the violence of a battle waged by undisciplined troops with a good deal of anger to vent. Perhaps this to some extent explains why the troops of Buddhist countries were described by Sangermano, and by other observers in terms similar to his, as 'dastardly in danger . . . and cruel in victory'.

'For king, religion cnd country'

We return therefore to the point from which we began this closer inspection of the South–East Asian Buddhist nations' record in peace and war, namely that loyalty to the state has come first and common interest with Buddhist co-religionists a poor second. Only on a very idealistic view would one have expected anything different. The record is strikingly similar to that of the Christian nations of Europe. Material interests proved stronger than ideal interests during the period when European Christian nations were competing for economic advantage, just as such interests did among South–East Asian Buddhist nations. The effective role of state religion was to reinforce the symbols of the state: 'for God, King and country' in England is paralleled by the slogan 'for king, religion and country' in Thailand. A reporter from Bangkok in March 1976 reported that this was still the cry (*Guardian*, London, 2 March 1976).

Appendix

On 18 October 1976, the Deputy Premier and Minister of Education, Sports and Religious Affairs in Laos, Phoumi Vong-vichit, addressed a gathering of Buddhist monks who were completing a 'training course' in Vientiane, the capital. His address dealt with the role the Communist government intended the Sangha to play in the new Laos. Some extracts from his address follow:

The Buddhist monks completing this course have learned several things which they were unable to study in the past. First they studied the Buddhist scriptures in Pali. . . . In addition, Buddhist monks can also study politics. Political study by Buddhist monks is obviously against a rule of the old regime which prohibited Buddhist monks from engaging in politics. . . . The study of politics by Buddhist monks is aimed at consolidating their political background so as to make it conform to progressive revolutionary politics. This study will enable Buddhist monks to integrate themselves more easily into the revolutionary ranks alongside revolutionary cadres.

[?Political study] is a good thing. First, it enables us to understand what politics is. Politics, as far as my understanding goes, is something which was practised by the Lord Buddha. It is a matter of human relationships; it views the current situation of the world, tells us what the world is, in what state the world is at present, why the world is like it is, and how we can improve it; and if we can improve the world, how and by what methods can we do it? This is what politics is about and, as I understand it, the Lord Buddha had a similar view.

While preparing to ascend the throne, the Lord Buddha thought of methods he was going to follow when taking control of the country. He came to understand that before administering the affairs of his kingdom, he should go to every corner of his country to find out the truth. When he saw the rich oppress and exploit the poor, he came to understand why that was so. When he saw high ranking court officials unjustly repress and intimidate other people, he also understood why. When he saw sick people sitting in their houses and public parks, he asked himself why the people got sick and why they were not cured. When he saw corpses in the jungles, he also asked himself why they died that way, whereas when the rich died, large cremations were performed for them. That was why he became unhappy. He came to understand that the world was that way because there was no justice in it. He then wondered whether such problems could be solved, and found out that they could. He asked himself how, and concluded that he had to seek the truth about all this. On learning the truth, he had to enter the monkhood so that he could give sermons and practise his teachings. It is difficult for a layman to teach laymen because laymen who are older than the teacher will not listen to or respect him. . . . Subsequently, the Lord Buddha gave up all his worldly possessions and became an ordinary person with only an alms bowl to beg food from other people. That meant that he tried to abolish the classes in his country and to create only one class – a class of morally conscious people who were respected by other people. It was in this way that the Lord Buddha became involved with politics. . . .

Why do human beings fail to live happily together on the earth? What are the duties of human beings on this earth? Human beings have nothing else to do but to carry out production for self-sufficiency. This is the only duty of human beings until they die. They have nothing else to do. That is why we hold that human beings must regard production as the most important task because it enables them to survive. . . .

We can see now that the revolutionary politics and the politics practised by the Lord Buddha have the same goals. They differ only in organization and practice. . . .

Politics develops according to circumstances in each period. . . . If science in the modern era is used to serve the classes advocating violence to forcibly repress the morally-conscious side, politics must protect the latter. We must understand this reality. I do not know whether politics was studied in this manner or not in Buddhist schools in the past. As far as I can see from reading the syllabus of Buddhist schools in the past politics was not thoroughly discussed and studied. As a result, certain Buddhist monks failed to understand political issues correctly.

In certain countries, Buddhist monks are prohibited from getting involved in or studying politics. I hold such prohibition to be a deprivation of the rights of Buddhist monks. Buddhist monks are political cadres of the Lord Buddha who are fighting injustice in the world. . . . Therefore, they must understand more profoundly their political duties.

It is worthy of note that Buddhism is practised in a different way in other countries. We should be proud that our understanding of Buddhism is different from that of other countries. . . . In certain countries, Buddhists practise meditation. Those who can meditate for a long time without food or sleep will command much respect from other Buddhist followers. Some can do that for five or seven consecutive days without any food or sleep. I think those who can fast for three months may go to their graves very soon. . . .

This is the first time that we have trained all-round Buddhist monk teachers in all respects. The training of such teachers will greatly benefit Buddhism in our country because it will help purify and make Buddhism in this country more scientific than in other countries. We have managed to allow a number of Buddhist monk teachers to rectify their old attitudes, adopt a new line of thinking and apply scientific knowledge to Buddhist politics, Buddhist theory and Buddhist philosophy. I believe that no other country has accomplished anything like this. . . .

The success of your study will benefit the nation because, as Buddhist monk teachers, you are now a resource for our country. You will now be able to correct some past mistakes in our society. You will become a group of political cadres who will closely co-operate with revolutionary political cadres in teaching and guiding our people to walk along the same path to the same destination, thereby making our nation more prosperous in future. . . . (100).

It is clear from this that the Sangha's importance as a much respected element in Laos society is recognised by the country's new rulers, such is the extent to which the Sangha has become an integral feature of the social and cultural structure. It might therefore have constituted a threat to a new political order, if its members were not given a new role and thus robbed of the opportunity to appear as martyrs leading a silent resistance movement. The attempt therefore had to be made to integrate them into the new machinery of the state. In a sense this development in Laos demonstrates the extent to which, in that country as elsewhere in South-East Asia, and notably in Thailand the Sangha had become an institution of the State, and one which had to be reckoned with in matters concerning social control, and could without much difficulty be enlisted by the State for its own purposes.

References

1	ACTS	*Acts of the Administration of the Buddhist Order of Sangha*, Mahamakut Educational Council, Bangkok, 1963.
2	A.E.R.I.	*Biruma no Keizai Kaihatsu* (English translation, *Economic Development in Burma*) Asian Economic Research Institute, Tokyo, 1961.
3	BA HAN	'The Emergence of the Burmese Nation', in *J.B.R.S.*, XLVIII, ii, December 1965.
4	BA MAW	*Breakthrough in Burma*, 1968.
5	BENNETT, Paul J.	*Conference under The Tamarind Tree : Three Essays in Burmese History*, 1971.
6	BIGANDET, P.	*The Life or Legend of Gaudama the Budha* (sic) *of the Burmese*, 1866.
7	BODE, Mabel Haynes	*The Pali Literature of Burma*, 1909.
8	BODE, Mabel Haynes	*Sasanavamsa* (Pali text, with Introduction) 1897.
9	BROWN, R. G.	*Burma as I Saw It*, 1926.
10	BRUCE, Helen	*Nine Temples of Bangkok*, 1960.
11	BULOW, Prince von	*Imperial Germany*, English edn, 1916.
12	BUTWELL, Richard	*U Nu of Burma*, 1969.
13	CADY, John	*A History of Modern Burma*, 1958.
14	CADY, John	*Thailand, Burma, Laos and Cambodia*, 1966.
15	CADY, John	*South East Asia : Its Historical Development*, 1964
16	COEDÈS, G.	*The Making of South–East Asia*, 1966.
17	COLLIS, Maurice	*Trials in Burma* (Penguin edition) 1945.
18	CROSTHWAITE, Sir Charles	*The Pacification of Burma*, 1912.
19	DHAMMASUDDHO, Bhikkhu	*The Story of Wat Bovoranives Vihara*, 1971.
20	DHANI NIVAT, H.H. Prince	*A History of Buddhism in Siam*, 1965.
21	DITTMAR, Johanna	*Thailand*, English translation by M.O'C. Walshe, 1971.
22	DODD, W. C.	*The Tai Race*, 1923.
23	DUTT,	*Buddhist India*, 1966.
24	FURNIVALL, J. S.	*Colonial Policy and Practice*, 1947.
25	GELLNER, Ernest	*Thought and Change*, 1974.

References

26	GREEN, Stephen	'King Wachirawut's Policy of Nationalism', in *In Memoriam : Phya Anuman Rajadhon*, ed. by Tej Bunnag and Michael Smithies, 1970.
27	HALL, D. G. E.	*A History of South–East Asia*, 3rd edn, 1968.
28	HALL, H. Fielding	*The Soul of a People*, 1898, 4th edn, 1902.
29	HARDY, R. Spence	*The British Government and the Idolatry of Ceylon*, 1841.
30	HARVEY, G. E.	*History of Burma*, 1925.
31	HARVEY, G. E.	'The Writing of Burmese History', in *J.B.R.S.* vol. IX, pt II, 1919.
32	HARVEY, G. E.	*British Rule in Burma 1824–1942*, 1946.
33	HAYDEN, Howard	*Higher Education and Development in South–East Asia*, vol. II, 1967.
34	HEINE-GELDERN, Robert von	*Conceptions of State and Kingship in South East Asia :* Data Paper No. 18, S.E. Asian Programme Cornell University, April 1956.
35	HTIN AUNG, Maung	*Folk Elements in Burmese Buddhism*, 1962.
36	HTIN AUNG, Maung	*Burmese Monk's Tales*, 1966.
37	HTIN AUNG, Maung	*A History of Burma*, 1967.
38	ISHII, Yoneo	'Church and State in Thailand', in *Asian Survey*, vol. 8, 1968, pp. 864–71.
39	JACOBS, Norman	*Modernization Without Development : Thailand as an Asian Case Study*, 1971.
40	JAYAWICKRAMA, N. A.	The Sheaf of Garlands of the Epochs of the Conqueror, being a translation of *Jinakalamalipakaranam*, 1968.
41	*Jinakalamali*	
42	J.M.B.S.	*Journal of the Maha Bodhi Society.*
43	JUMSAI, M. L. Manich	*Popular History of Thailand*, 1972.
44	JUMSAI, M. L. Manich	*History of Thai Literature*, 1973.
45	KAUNG, U.	'A Survey of the History of Education in Burma before the British Conquest and after', in *Journal of the Burma Research Society*, vol. XLVI, part II, December 1963.
46	KEYES, Charles F.	'Buddhism and National Integration in Thailand', in *Journal of Asian Studies*, vol. 30, no. 3, 1971.
47	KIERNAN, V. G.	*Marxism and Imperialism*, 1974.
48	LACH, Donald F.	*South East Asia in the Eyes of Europe : Sixteenth Century*, 1968.
49	LANDON, Kenneth P.	*Siam in Transition*, 1939.
50	LING, Trevor O.	*Buddhism and the Mythology of Evil*, 1962.
51	LING, Trevor O.	*The Buddha : Buddhist Civilization in India and Ceylon*, 1973 (Pelican edition 1976).
52	LING, Trevor O.	'Buddhist Factors in Population Growth and

		Control', in *Population Studies*, vol. XXIII, pt 1, March 1969.
53	LINGAT, R.	'History of Wat Pavaranivesa', in *J.S.S.*, 1932.
54	LE MAY, R.	*The Cultures of South–East Asia*, 1956.
55	LUCE, G. H.	'The Mons of the Pagan Dynasty', a lecture to Rangoon University Mon Society, January 1950.
56	LUCE, G. H.	'The Ancient Pyu', in *Journal of the Burma Research Society*, vol. XXVII, no. iii, 1937.
57	MAHAMAKUT	*Buddhist Education in Thailand*, Mahamakut Educational Council, Bangkok, 1961.
58	MAHAVAMSA	
59	MARASINGHE, M. M. J.	*Gods in Early Buddhism*, 1974.
60	M.B.U.B.W.	*Maha Bodhi and the United Buddhist World*, periodical publication.
61	MENDELSON, E. Michael	'Buddhism and the Burmese Establishment' in *Archives de Sociologie des Religions*, vol. 17, 1964.
62	MENDELSON, E. Michael	'A Messianic Buddhist Association in Upper Burma', in *Bulletin of the School of Oriental and African Studies*, London, vol. 24, 1961.
63	MENDELSON E. Michael	'The King of the Weaving Mountain', in *Royal Central Asian Journal*, vol. 48, 1961.
64	MENDELSON, E. Michael	'Observations on a Tour in the Region of Mount Popa, Central Burma', in *France-Asie*, vol. 179, 1963.
65	MENDELSON, E. Michael	'The Uses of Religious Scepticism in Burma', in *Diogenes*, vol. 41, 1963.
66	MENDELSON, E. Michael	*Sangha and State in Burma*, 1976.
67	MOSCOTTI, Albert D.	*British Policy and the Nationalist Movement in Burma 1917–1937*, 1974.
68	MYA MAUNG	'Cultural Values and Economic Change in Burma', in *Man, State and Society in Contemporary South–East Asia*, ed. by R. O. Tilman, 1969.
69	NARASU, P. Lakshmi	*The Essence of Buddhism*, 1907.
70	NICHOLAS, C. W. and PARANAVITANA, S.	*A Concise History of Ceylon*, Colombo, 1961.
71	NASH, June C.	'Living with Nats: An Analysis of Animism in Burmese Village Social Relations', in *Anthropological Studies in Theravada Buddhism*, ed. by Manning Nash, 1966.
72	NASH, Manning	*The Golden Road to Modernity: Village Life in Contemporary Burma*, 1969.

References

73	NEEDHAM, Rodney	*Belief, Language and Experience,* 1972.
74	NISBET, J.	*Burma under British Rule and Before,* 2 vols, 1901.
75	NU, U	*U Nu Saturday's Son* (translated by U Law Yone), 1975.
76	NYANATILOKA	*Dictionary of Buddhism,* 1956.
77	PANNASAMI	See *Sasanavamsa.*
78	PENDLETON, Robert G.	*Thailand : Aspects of Landscape and Life,* 1963.
79	PHILLIPS, Herbert	*Thai Peasant Personality,* 1965.
80	PHILLIPS, Herbert	'The Culture of Siamese Intellectuals', in *Change and Persistence in Thai Society,* ed. by G. William Skinner and A. Thomas Kirsch, 1975.
81	PURCHAS, Samuel	*His Pilgrimage, or Relations of the World and the Religions,* London, 1616.
82	PYE, Lucian W.	*Politics, Personality and Nation Building,* 1962.
83	RAY, Nihar-Ranjan	*An Introduction to the study of Theravada Buddhism in Burma,* Calcutta, 1946.
84	SADDHATISSA, H.	*Upasakajanalankara : A Critical Edition and Study,* 1965.
85	SANGERMANO, Father	*A Description of the Burmese Empire,* translated into English by William Tandy, Rangoon, 1924 (reprinted London 1966).
86	SARKISYANZ, E.	*Buddhist Backgrounds of the Burmese Revolution,* 1965.
87	SASANASOBHON, Phra	*His Majesty King Rama the Fourth Mongkut,* Bangkok, 1968.
88	*Sasanavamsa* or:	*The History of the Buddha's Religion* by Pannasami, translated by B. C. Law (Sacred Books of the East, vol. XVII) 1952.
89	SATYAMURTHY, T. V.	'Some Aspects of Burmese Nationalism', in *Nationalism, Revolution and Evolution in South–East Asia,* ed. by Michael Leifer, 1970.
90	SCHUMACHER, E. F.	'Buddhist Economics', in *Asia : A Handbook* (ed. by Guy Wint), 1965.
91	SCOTT, J. G.	*Burma as It Was, as It Is, and as It Will Be,* 1886.
92	SEIDENFADEN, Erik	*The Thai Peoples,* 1963.
93	SIFFIN, William J.	*The Thai Bureaucracy,* 1966.
94	SINGHAL, D. P.	*The Annexation of Upper Burma,* 1960.
95	SMITH, Donald Eugene	*Religion, Politics and Social Change in the Third World,* 1971.
96	SMITH, Donald Eugene	*Religion and Politics in Burma,* 1965.

97	SPIRO, Melford E.	*Buddhism and Society,* 1971.
98	SUKSAMRAN, Somboon	*Political Buddhism in South–East Asia,* 1977.
99	SYMANANDA, Rong	*A History of Thailand,* 1971.
100	SUMMARY OF WORLD BROADCASTS, 1 November 1976, FE/5352/B/6–8.	
101	TAMBIAH, S. J.	*Buddhism and the Spirit Cults in North–East Thailand,* 1970.
102	TAMBIAH, S. J.	*World Conqueror and World Renouncer,* 1976.
103	THAN TUN	'Social Life in Burma, 1044–1287', in *J.B.R.S.,* vol. XLI, December 1958.
104	THAN TUN	'A History of Burma' (serialised), in *New Burma Weekly,* 1959.
105	THAPAR, R.	*Asoka and the Decline of the Mauryas,* 1961.
106	THOMPSON, J. S.	'Marxism in Burma', in *Marxism in South–East Asia,* ed. by Frank N. Trager, 1959.
107	THOMPSON, V.	*Thailand; the New Siam,* 1941.
108	THOMPSON, V. and ADLOFF, R.	*Minority Problems in South–East Asia,* 1955.
109	TINKER, Hugh	*The Union of Burma,* 4th edn, 1967.
110	TOTTEN, George O.	'Buddhism and Socialism in Japan and Burma', in *Comparative Studies in Society and History,* vol. 2, 1959–60.
111	TOWLER, R.	*Homo Religiosus: Sociological Problems in the Study of Religion,* 1974.
112	TRAGER, Frank N.	*Burma from Kingdom to Republic,* 1966.
113	TRAGER, Helen G.	*Burma through alien eyes: Missionary views of the Burmese in the nineteenth century,* London, 1966.
114	VAN DER MEHDEN, Fred R.	*Religion and Nationalism in South–East Asia,* 1963.
115	VELLA, Walter F.	*Siam under Rama III,* New York, 1957.
116	WALES, H. G. Quaritch	*Dvaravati: The Earliest Kingdom of Siam,* 1969.
117	WALINSKY, Louis J.	*Economic Development in Burma, 1951–60,* 1962.
118	WARREN, C. U.	*Burmese Interlude,* 1937.
119	WEBER, Max	*The Religion of India: The Sociology of Hinduism and Buddhism,* 1958.
120	WEBER, Max	*Sociology of Religion* (translated by E. Fisschoff), 1963.
121	WELLS, K. E.	*Thai Buddhism: Its Rites and Activities,* 1960.
122	WHITE, H. Thirkell	*A Civil Servant in Burma,* 1913.
123	WOOD, W. A. R.	*A History of Siam,* 1924.
124	YULE, Henry	*Narrative of the Mission to the Court of Ava in 1855,* London, 1858.

Glossary

Abhidhamma see *Tipitaka*

Bhikkhu commonly translated 'monk'. This is inaccurate to the extent that it suggests a life cut off from the world. The Pali word bhikkhu (Sanskrit *bhikshu*) means literally a 'sharer', that is a share of the lay people's meal is set aside for him. In Burma the bhikkhu is called '*hpon-gyi*' (pronounced 'pone' to rhyme with bone, and 'jee') meaning 'great glory'. In Thailand he is called '*phra*', a title for one who is highly honoured.

Bodhisattva one who is in the process of becoming Buddha, in the sense of being in the penultimate stage; such a being then holds back from the final stage in order to help others by means of the great spiritual power he has gained. Such beings have become associated with 'gods' in Indian culture, and have also been associated with kingship, in Burma, for example.

Buddha An 'enlightened' or 'awakened' one, who upon becoming enlightened teaches others the truth into which he has entered. What he thus teaches is the Dhamma (q.v.).

Dhamma (Pali). In Sanskrit, Dharma. The word has many distinguishable meanings, of which the most important in Buddhist terminology is that which is taught by the Buddha (q.v.).

Jatakas 'Birth-stories', that is the stories of former existences or 'births' mainly of Gotama Buddha. These are old Indian folk tales adapted to suit Buddhist purposes, and given a Buddhist identification. There are various different collections of them in the Theravada countries. The Sinhalese Pali canonical collection consists of 547 separate stories, some long and some short. Certain Jatakas have traditionally been more popular, and lists of ten or more of these are found in the different Buddhist countries of South–East Asia.

Nikaya A major collection of 'suttas', or discourses. The Sutta Pitaka (see Tipitaka) consists of five Nikayas.

Pagoda see *Stupa*

Phra see *Bhikkhu*

Pongyi see *Bhikkhu*

Pongyi-chaung see *Vihara*

Samsara the 'stream' of mortal existences, in which birth takes place again and again until the 'further shore' is reached, and continued rebirth (and continued-dying) is no more.

Sangha The 'assembly', or fraternity, or order of Buddhist monks (bhikkhus).

Sasana literally, the discipline, or rule of life; thus, the 'Buddha-sasana' is the way of life followed by the devotee of the Buddha. The term is often translated in the broad sense of (Buddhist) religion.

Shaiva, Shaivite Pertaining to Shiva, one of the major Hindu deities; cf. Vaishnava.

Stupa A memorial mound, used in ancient India to honour great kings. Adopted by Buddhists as shrine for relics, such as ashes or bones of deceased Buddhist saints. In its developed form in Indian and South–East Asia is often called a *pagoda*, and in Thailand a *chedi*, with the original dome shape extended upwards to a point, covered with a 'hti', or small, umbrella-like cover.

Thera, Theravada literally 'an elder' or senior bhikkhu. The doctrine of such 'seniors' is their *vada*; hence the Theravada is the name of one of the eighteen schools which together went to make up the non-Mahayanist wing, the Hinayana.

Tipitaka The complete Pali Buddhist canonical scriptures. Ti (three) Pitaka (baskets, because the whole consists of three separate collections:
(1) the *Suttas* or 'discourses', mainly of the Buddha;
(2) the *Vinaya* or code of discipline, for monks, which includes also some long narrative passages about the history of the Sangha; and
(3) the *Abhidhamma*, or abstract of the doctrine, consisting of lists and tables, and schemes of classification of mental events, their different possible combinations etc.

Vaishnava, Vaishnavite Pertaining to *Vishnu* one of the major Hindu deities; hence a worshipper of Vishnu and the company of such worshippers. The hybrid form 'Vaishnavite' is used in the same sense.

Vihara A dwelling place for bhikkhus (q.v.), often including also preaching halls for lay people, and a stupa, and hence sometimes translated broadly as 'monastery'. In Thailand the word *wat* is used in the same sense for such a complex. In Burma it is called a 'pongyi-chaung', i.e. a 'chaung' or building for pongyis, q.v.

Wat see *Vihara*

Index

Index

Index

Index